Best Soft Fruit

Stefan Buczacki
Best Soft Fruit

HAMLYN

Executive Art Editor Robin Whitecross
Executive Editor Anna Mumford
Designer Michael Whitehead
Editor Isobel Holland
Production Sarah Rees
Picture Research Jenny Faithfull

First published in Great Britain in 1994
by Hamlyn an imprint of Reed Consumer Books Limited
Michelin House, 81 Fulham Road, London SW3 6RB
and Auckland, Melbourne, Singapore and Toronto

Reprinted 1994

© Reed International Books Limited 1994
Text © Stefan Buczacki 1994
Design © Reed Consumer Books 1994

Produced by Butler & Tanner
Printed in Frome, Somerset

ISBN 0 600 57733 3

A catalogue of this book is available at the British Library

CONTENTS

INTRODUCTION

The first feature that I created in my present garden was the soft fruit area; and I really think that it is the last that I would part with. But as gardeners are sometimes still confused over which fruit are 'soft' and which not, I must start with a brief explanation.

Protected raspberry canes growing alongside the vegetable patch

A haze of lavender acts as a foil to a row of cordon-trained gooseberries

DEFINITION OF SOFT FRUIT

Most fruit, when they are ripe, are pretty soft, otherwise they would be unpalatable. I suppose that a more practical division, therefore, might be between those fruit that grow on trees and those fruit that grow on bushes and canes. So you would have apples, pears, plums and their kind, known as top fruit, on the one hand and currants, gooseberries, blueber- ries, raspberries, blackberries and their kin, called soft fruit, on the other. This is a more useful grouping and it becomes even more meaning- ful when it is borne in mind that the bush and cane fruits are shorter-lived than the tree types. So we can then, with justification, add the even shorter-lived or annual fruits such as strawberries, melons and Cape gooseberries. It still leaves a couple of oddities: two climbing plants that are certainly long-lived but which produce fruit that I feel are fairly close in flavour and use to conven- tional 'soft fruits', the grape and the Chinese gooseberry or Kiwi fruit.

SELF-FERTILE PLANTS

Something else of practical value is shared by almost all soft fruits, and in this they differ from most top fruits: they are self-fertile. This means that only one plant or, more usually in practice, only one variety, is needed to obtain a crop. So there is my more or less logical list of soft fruit, and I believe all are fairly easy, and some very easy, to grow. It's true that not every one of them can be grown in all gardens because of site or soil condi- tions, but I don't believe there is any garden that can't manage some of them. And this is true even of small plots, for the odd soft fruit plant can be fitted into very little space and even if it won't give you fruit for more than a few helpings, they will certainly be splendid, fresh helpings.

USING THIS BOOK

Each type of soft fruit is described individually in chapters which should give you all the information neces- sary to select the best types and to grow them successfully. From the numerous varieties available, I have highlighted and illustrated those that I consider the most suitable all round choice for most gardens. In the introductory pages 8-35 how- ever, I have given general advice on such features as soil preparation, fertilizers and pest and disease con- trol which should be read in con- junction with each chapter.

A bird's eye view of a neatly planned and well-laid out soft fruit growing area

CHOOSING THE SITE

It is most important, for the reasons I've indicated, that you choose a site in your garden that provides the optimum requirements for the successful growing of soft fruit.

No fruit is of much use unless it is fairly sweet. And although the optimum sweetness of, for example, a ripe Kiwi fruit will be less than that of a melon, there is no doubt that the sugar content of any fruit will be higher if it is grown in warm sun than if it is grown in shade. This is not to ignore that in their wild states, many soft fruits are woodland plants; raspberries and strawberries, for instance, grow naturally in the dappled light of clearings among forest trees. But anyone who has collected

A small bed of srawberry plants is the perfect partner for a large and productive vegetable garden

wild fruits will know that, almost without exception, they are less sweet and certainly smaller than their cultivated counterparts. In passing, I might add that their flavour may be as good or better, but that is a variety characteristic whereas sweetness depends chiefly on warmth.

SUNNY SITE

My advice therefore, all things being equal, is that you should choose the warmest, sunniest part of your garden for growing your soft fruit. Of course, all things won't always be equal, for the sunniest spot may be in front of your living room windows and, as you will probably wish to grow most of your soft fruit (and certainly most of the cane and bush plants) inside some form of protective cage (see p.24), they won't necessarily be particularly ornamental. Overall size of the area will also dictate its positioning and on p.14, I have suggested two fruit garden plans to give an idea of how much space might be involved. In passing, I should mention that whilst most soft fruit are normally grown, and certainly all *can* be grown outdoors in a temperate climate, a greenhouse is

A grapevine growing against a wall in a well protected and sunny site

desirable for melons, Cape gooseberries and grapes.

SHELTER

After sunshine, shelter from wind is the most important factor. No type of soft fruit will tolerate strong, cold winds and none are really successful in coastal areas subject to a great deal of salt spray. For the climbing fruits, shelter will generally be provided by the wall against which they are trained. For the others, a garden fence or wall will usually suffice, bearing in mind the need to position the plants facing the sun. Placing a soft fruit area close to a hedge, especially a fairly rough hedge of native plants is not, however, a very good plan as it is likely to harbour pest and disease organisms.

CHANGE OF LOCATION

Fortunately, once chosen, the soft-fruit plot for most types of plant will function for up to about 10 years before new plants and a new location

are required. Then, as with any type of plant that has grown in the same place for a number of years, it's sensible, if at all possible, to move to a new spot with different soil. I suppose the most problematic soft fruits from this point of view are strawberries, which are much shorter term prospects and are really best rotated in a similar manner to vegetables. On p.87, I've discussed the best ways to manage a strawberry bed.

CLEARING THE SITE

Time taken in clearing and preparing the site for soft fruit growing is always time well spent. Perennial weeds are especially important and if it takes a few weeks of using a translocated weedkiller to remove couch grass, bindweed and similar deep-seated weeds, so be it; the benefits will be appreciated over the many years that the fruit garden is in place.

WIND PROTECTION

Protection from the wind is most important. First because its sheer physical force may uproot plants or at least rock them in the ground and so affect their root function; second because its constant drying effect will draw excessive amounts of water from plants and so stunt their growth, and third because it will blow away both pollen and pollinating insects, resulting in a poorer crop.

SOIL

With two very significant exceptions, the preferred soil for all types of soft fruit is similar and can be satisfied in most gardens. A well drained medium loam with a pH of around 6.5 (that is, one just on the acidic side of neutral) is ideal. In general, a soil that is slightly wetter than this will naturally produce better crops than one that is on the dry side, but both can be improved by digging in quantities of well rotted manure, compost or other organic matter.

Blueberries will flourish only if grown in very acidic soil

A dry soil is, of course, a soil short of water and as it is water that causes soft fruit to be soft, those produced on drier sites tend to be small, hard and tasteless. On naturally heavier, wetter soils (which also tend to be colder), you are likely to achieve the best success with black-currants, followed by raspberries, blackberries and related hybrid berries; as much as anything because they are more tolerant of the root-rotting fungi that are prevalent in wet conditions.

SOIL pH

Problems will occur with most soft fruit, and especially with raspberries and strawberries, when they are grown in a chalky soil. This is because the important element, iron, is difficult for plants to take up in alkaline conditions. Iron is needed in the manufacture of the green photo-synthesis chemical, chlorophyll. Iron shortage causes chlorosis which is manifest as the development of pale coloured leaves with dark green veins. Because of the shortage of chlorophyll, the leaves and the plant as a whole fail to function properly. It's very difficult to acidify a naturally chalky soil and when the pH is very high (above about 8.0), soft fruit growing will be particularly difficult. In only slightly alkaline conditions, however, it makes sense to apply sequestered iron once a year in spring. This is iron in an organic form that can more readily be taken up by plants from chalky conditions, and several specially formulated propri-etary fertilizers provide this.

ACID SOIL FRUITS

The exceptional soft fruit to which I

WEED CONTROL

Even if all weeds have been removed before the fruit garden is established, it's an inescapable fact that more will grow but they must be kept under control if the fruit plants are to give of their best. Persistent weedkillers must not be used because they will remain in the soil and damage the fruit but non-persistent total weedkillers such as the translo-cated chemical glyphosate or the widely used proprietary

contact mixture of paraquat and diquat are perfectly safe if applied exactly as the manufacturers direct. Glyphosate will be needed for deep rooted perennial weeds and a con-tact weedkiller for annual or seedling weeds, although I only use chemical control for annual weeds when the soil is very damp and unsuitable for hoeing. And of course, the organic mulch placed close to the plants to retain soil moisture will also be beneficial in keeping annual weeds in check close to the plants referred above are blueberries and cranberries. These are often grouped together, as I have done, under the name 'acid soil fruits'; the term 'heathland fruits' is also sometimes used. The conditions they require are truly those of a natural peat-rich heathland; extreme acidity, with a pH as low as 4.0 or even 3.5. Unless your soil is naturally of this type, therefore, it is not worth trying to grow these plants, any more than it's worth trying rhododendrons, azaleas and summer-flowering heathers.

A healthy crop of blackcurrants growing in rich, well-maintained soil

SOIL IMPROVEMENT

I have said on many occasions that time and effort spent on improving your garden soil will never be regretted. But 'improvement' doesn't mean the same thing to all gardeners so perhaps I should outline what can and should be done to soil and what can't and shouldn't be attempted. By and large, while soil structure can be changed, soil texture cannot. For texture is an expression of the relative amounts of sand, silt and clay particles that the soil contains. You can add many tons of sand to your garden soil but it will be, to use a familiar metaphor, just a drop in the ocean. Soil structure however expresses the manner in which these particles are associated with organic matter or humus to produce a blend of larger, pellet-like crumbs with holes or pores between. And by adding organic matter, you can certainly increase both the number of pores and crumbs, a process that paradoxically will increase the moisture retentiveness of a free-draining sandy soil just as readily as it will improve the drainage of a heavy clay.

Organic matter can be added to soil as a surface mulch, a beneficial enough process in itself that cuts down water loss through evaporation and suppresses weed growth. In due course, worms will drag down the surface mulch into the body of the soil. But as a method of adding large quantities of organic matter, double digging is far more efficient, although of course this can only be done in advance of planting, not among established bushes.

TOOLS AND EQUIPMENT

Most of the tools and items of equipment you need for growing soft fruit successfully will be familiar to you. Indeed, you probably have many of them already. But the methods involved in using them may not be so well known, even to otherwise experienced gardeners. Soft fruit growing is a very precise art and, although many of the procedures involved are similar, say, to the cultivation of flowering shrubs, the aim is, obviously, to obtain the best crops. This means that your familiar procedures and disciplines have to be followed just that bit more strictly, and you will almost certainly need some quite specific pieces of equipment.

You will, of course, be aiming to produce a fine crop of sweet, appetizing fruit and if you succeed, there may be fierce competition for the end result. Rather than letting the early bird get the raspberry, protect your crops all year round, ideally with a permanent fruit cage the sides and top of which should be formed of netting with a mesh of 1.3-2cm (½-1in). Your cage can be a home-made affair or based on a modular kit to provide exactly the size of structure you need. Wall-trained fruits can be protected with lightweight netting draped over them, as can strawberries, but birds have been known to peck fruit through the mesh so, if possible, hold the net away from the strawberries with a system of bamboo canes topped with upturned plastic flowerpots. Also useful for

Raffia is ideal for tying-in branches

protecting strawberries is heavy gauge black plastic sheet, admittedly more functional than decorative, spread over the strawberry bed and held firmly in place with the plants inserted through small slits and planted directly into the ground below. This takes the place of straw mulch or strawberry mats, and has the further advantage of keeping the soil warm and moist. This tough plastic sheet can also be used to line the sides of a raspberry trench to reduce suckering too far from the supports (see p.89).

SUPPORT

Support and training takes on a far greater importance in the soft fruit garden than in other situations. To provide the really solid structures that most cane and climbing fruit need, you will need 2.3m (8ft) wooden posts — I favour the round, rustic, pressure treated type, with a spike at the bottom — driven into the ground to a depth of about 45-60cm (18-24in) with a further 1.8m (6ft) above ground. Bracing these

A selection of well-cared-for tools

with shorter stakes, driven into the ground at an angle and bolted securely is worthwhile, as the additional stability it brings is tremendous. Stretched between the uprights you will need heavy-duty galvanized or plastic-covered wire, preferably 10-gauge, attached to bolts, vine-eyes or adjustable straining bolts. And to tie your canes in, make sure you always carry with you a ball of soft garden twine or raffia and a pair of scissors or a knife.

PROPAGATION

For propagation, particularly from seed, a heated propagator can be helpful although many gardeners manage perfectly well with windowsills, airing cupboards and other make-shift methods. For growing dessert grapes and melons in quantity, you really need a greenhouse, and a fairly sizeable one. Smaller quantities of melons can be grown quite successfully in cold frames or even plastic and glass cloches, which can also be invaluable for bringing on an early crop of strawberries.

WATERING EQUIPMENT

Succulent, juicy fruit means regular and plentiful watering. The humble watering can will deliver water just where you want it, but for large fruit gardens or absentee gardeners a sprinkler or, preferably, trickle irrigation system will be extremely helpful. There will certainly be times when you want to deliver liquid feed along with the water, so choose a dilutor that allows you to do this.

TOOLS FOR PRUNING

Pruning is extremely important in getting the best from your soft fruit. A pair of sharp, well-maintained and regularly cleaned anvil-type secateurs will deal with most canes, but for tougher jobs, long handled loppers, again anvil-type, are ideal. For cutting back strawberry foliage at the end of the season, I favour a pair of single-handed shears. Blunt-ended scissors are essential, not only because they won't cut holes in pockets, but because they are less likely to damage gooseberries or grapes when you are picking or thinning the fruit. A pair of strong, leather-palmed gardening gloves should go some way to protecting your hands from spiny stems and canes, and for pulling up raspberry suckers, they are a must. A stainless-steel spade will make site preparation easy, and is useful for preparing slit trenches for hardwood cuttings, while your border fork comes in useful for spreading an organic mulch around plants in spring and autumn. Use a hoe for shallow weeding between rows of canes or bushes, and for removing raspberry suckers. A hand trowel is needed for planting strawberries. Fruits, like Kiwi fruit, that need a little help with pollination are best served with a soft paintbrush.

CONTAINER GROWING

In limited space, many types of soft fruit can be grown in containers, the larger the better. Wooden half-barrels, lined with plastic to minimize rotting of the wood, or large terracotta pots look best. Large plastic pots lose less water, but never really manage to look like anything but plastic, while strawberry pots, although certainly space saving, take a good deal of watering, feeding and general maintenance. Soil-based composts provide a reasonable supply of nutrients, and their weight gives extra stability to plastic containers. Container growing may be the only way to grow acid-loving fruits in an area with neutral to alkaline soil. Use ericaceous compost, make sure you irrigate with stored rainwater, and use conifer sawdust as a mulch. Mulching with well rotted organic matter or pulverized bark twice yearly, in spring and autumn, when the soil is already moist, can help retain soil water even in periods of reduced rainfall, while a straw mulch under strawberries to lift them slightly from the soil reduces the likelihood of fungus damage.

PEST CONTROL

Despite preventive measures of this kind, it is almost inevitable that you will have to spray at some point. Whether with fungicide, insecticide or herbicide, follow the manufacturer's instructions, never mix different products unless specified in the instructions, and store chemicals in their original containers under lock and key. Once chemicals have been diluted, they generally do not last long, so only make up as much as you need for one application. Clearly label your plastic sprayers, and keep one specifically for each type of chemical. Precautions for storing garden chemicals should be extended to fertilizers too. Above all, keep them dry and use them up reasonably quickly as they can loose their potency fairly rapidly.

Even the more gruelling of gardening tasks can be made less irksome by using well-made and comfortable-to-handle tools

PLANNING A SOFT FRUIT GARDEN

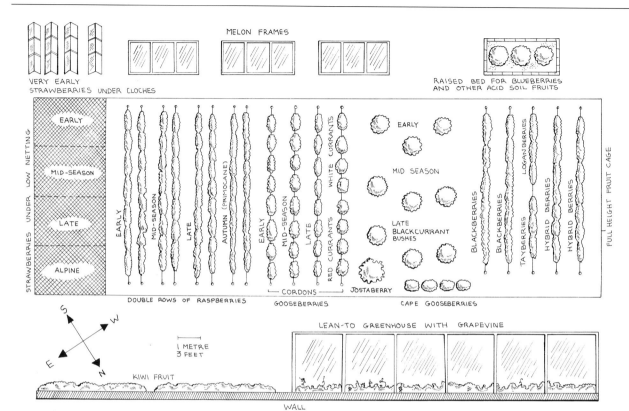

A clear and detailed visual plan of the ideal large fruit garden, (above) a plan for a smaller garden, (right)

If you are lucky enough to be able to create a new soft fruit garden, it is most important before you do anything to sit down and consider all the factors involved.

PLAN FOR A LARGE FRUIT GARDEN

The positioning of any large garden plot, be it for soft fruit, vegetables or ornamentals must inevitably be a compromise between the different requirements of each individual type of plant being grown. However, I would stress what I consider to be the most important factor for the soft fruit garden: the closer that your site can come to facing the sun whilst also offering adequate shelter from cold winds, the better. For grapevines, Kiwi fruit, Cape gooseberries and melons, some protective structure in the shape either of a greenhouse or cold frame is very desirable but I accept that it may not be possible to integrate this fully into the remainder of the area in the way that I have indicated on the above plan. For the greenhouse in particular, the value of proximity to a building should perhaps weigh most heavily in your planning.

Another problem that should not be ignored is that of access, particularly in such a large area. It is important to lay an infrastructure of pathways so that you don't have to clamber through one planted area to reach another. Paths and gateways should be wide enough to allow wheelbarrows to pass through and if, like me, you prefer to have walkways of grass in some parts of the fruit garden, do be sure that they are wide enough for your lawnmower!

PLAN FOR A SMALL FRUIT GARDEN

Special considerations apply to a small fruit garden. Your choice of varieties is paramount, for you will simply not be able to indulge in the luxury of early, mid-season and later fruiting types of soft fruit. Select those with the longest cropping period or, conversely, those that freeze most satisfactorily in order to obtain value and use from your produce over the longest possible period. If your garden is very small and your space very limited, there is of course no reason why even a small collection of fruit such as those I have shown in my plan couldn't be split up, with raspberries, for instance, in one spot and blackcurrants in another. The obvious drawback to this approach is that you will be unlikely to be able to provide proper protection from the birds. Simply throwing lightweight plastic netting over the plants will offer a degree of protection but is scarcely likely to enhance the aesthetic appeal of your garden. Ultimately, therefore, you may have to compromise between the possibility of losing a proportion of your crop and not being able to grow your chosen selection of soft fruit plants.

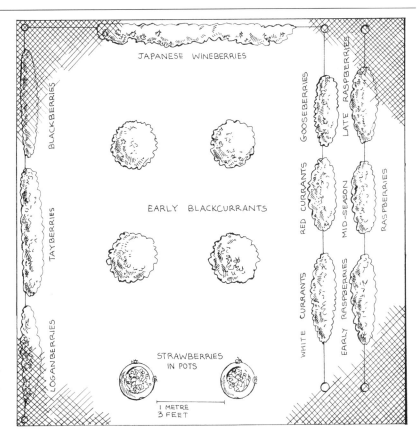

JAPANESE WINEBERRIES

BLACKBERRIES

GOOSEBERRIES

LATE RASPBERRIES

EARLY BLACKCURRANTS

TAYBERRIES

RED CURRANTS

MID-SEASON

RASPBERRIES

LOGANBERRIES

WHITE CURRANTS

EARLY RASPBERRIES

STRAWBERRIES
IN POTS

1 METRE
3 FEET

A tranquil and picturesque garden plan, which combines both soft fruit and vegetables most successfully

BUYING AND PLANTING

With the odd exception of the melon, a few types of strawberry and the Cape gooseberry, all of which are raised from seed, soft fruit will always be bought as young plants, generally under three years of age.

I'm convinced that obtaining stock of high quality is probably more important with soft fruit than with almost any other type of garden plant. Of course, any plant will be healthier, stronger and will establish better if it has been well grown by a competent nurseryman. But with soft fruit plants that are routinely propagated vegetatively (by cuttings, grafts or division, rather than by seed), it is probable that the progeny will acquire any virus contamination present in the tissues of the parent. Virus contamination results in an enfeebled plant and a lower yield. It's essential, therefore, that the plants are propagated from virus-free stock whenever this is available and whether you buy by mail order from a specialist fruit plant supplier or from a garden centre, do be sure that virus-free propagating material has been used. Generally, details in the catalogue, the individual label on the plant or, in a garden centre, a label close to where the plants are standing should tell you this. Resist the temptation to buy cut-price offers from anonymous suppliers and, for once, don't accept your neighbour's generous offer of his or her suckers or cuttings.

CERTIFICATION SCHEME

The most extensive and sophisticated certification scheme for virus-free fruit plants operates in Great

Bare-rooted raspberry canes, recently heeled-in, awaiting planting

Britain but virus-free quality assurance is also available in other countries. The British scheme involves three types of grading certificate:

'Special Stock' comprises the healthiest stock available, propagated from plants that have been obtained from an official research organisation and were virus-free at that time. Usually, such very high grade plants are used only for further propagation or for establishing commercial plantations. They are rarely offered to gardeners.

'A' Certificate plants are those that have, themselves, been propagated from 'Special Stock' Certificate material and the majority of virus-free plants sold to gardeners will be of this grade. Most modern blackcurrant, raspberry and strawberry varieties, as well as tayberries, tummelberries, sunberries, the red currant variety 'Redstart' and the

gooseberry varieties 'Invicta' and 'Jubilee' are both obtainable with 'A' certification.

'H' Certificate plants should only be purchased when 'A' Certificate stock isn't available. They are plants bred outside the UK and now being grown in Britain for the first time, or alternatively are plants that have been micro-propagated, a process that entails the growing of plantlets, initially under laboratory conditions, from tiny portions of tissue.

'Medana' a rather puzzling prefix is attached to a few fruit varieties, most notably tayberries. This is a registered trademark indicating that the variety was raised at a British government research institute and that a royalty payment to the institute is involved.

A GOOD SUPPLIER

For fruit varieties such as white currants, many hybrid berries, blueber-

Planting out a young strawberry plant

PLANTING

Bare-rooted plants must be planted promptly or heeled in – planted temporarily in a shallow hole with the roots well covered in soil. Container plants can be planted when convenient. Although I have described specific planting techniques and needs in the individual entries (blackcurrants, for instance, should always be planted deeply and raspberries are best planted in a trench), always remember that the soil must be well prepared with organic matter and a phosphate-rich fertilizer such as bone meal, and that the planting hole should be roughly twice the volume of the root ball. The roots of bare-rooted plants should be spread out carefully and uniformly while the compost around container-grown plants should be gently teased away. In many instances, the shoot growth should be cut back if this hasn't already been done by the nursery, but it is almost always advantageous with bare-rooted plants to trim back the roots lightly too. This will encourage new fibrous root development and so help rapid establishment. I have also always been an advocate of 'watering-in' a newly planted plant, not simply with water but with a solution of liquid fertilizer; again to encourage rapid establishment and aid recovery from transplanting shock. Always slope the soil away from the stem base after planting. This encourages the water to run away from the stem and not collect at the base. Finish by topping up with an organic mulch.

ries, cranberries and Kiwi fruit, not included in a certification scheme, I can only repeat my advice to buy from a reputable supplier whose credibility is established through him or her supplying certified stock of other types of soft fruit.

HOW PLANTS ARE SUPPLIED

Although individual requirements vary slightly between different types of soft fruit, the old adage that if a plant is given a good start, it will succeed better has a certain truth. In general, all soft fruit will be supplied either bare-rooted or growing in containers. Together with roses, soft fruit plants are probably supplied more frequently by mail order than other types of plant; and in general they will be sent during the dormant season, bare-rooted. The plants will have been dug straight from the nursery bed and packed in hessian or plastic wrapping, usually with some moisture-retaining material such as moss or straw. When bought from garden centres or personally from nurseries, they will almost invariably be growing in a soilless compost in a plastic container.

An established and healthy 'A' certificate 'Jubilee' gooseberry

FOOD AND WATER

The key to soft, succulent and tasty fruit is adequate moisture (after all, a large proportion of the volume of any fruit is water) and appropriate nutrients. In addition to sunshine and warmth, it is usually a shortage of water and appropriate food that makes for disappointing crops in gardens.

I stress *appropriate* food, for it's important to appreciate the differences between the role that each nutrient plays. In very simple terms, nitrogen encourages the growth of leaves and other green parts, a most important attribute because only green tissue can photosynthesize and so lead to vigorous growth overall. Phosphate is most important in stimulating root development which means secure anchorage and the effective uptake of mineral substances from the soil, while potash encourages flower and fruit formation. For a fruiting plant therefore, the value of potash is self-evident but it is important to achieve the correct balance, with sufficient nitrogen being given to ensure that the plant as a whole is strong and vigorous, but not in such large doses that the foliage develops at the expense of the fruit.

FEEDING

Although commercial fruit growers use rather complicated feeding regimes for each type of fruit plant (and sometimes, even for individual varieties), far less critical standards are needed in gardens. Over the years, I have found that my soft fruit garden needs are satisfied by two principal fertilizers and the advice in the individual entries is based around these. A balanced general fertilizer, applied once a year will be perfectly adequate to produce good

soft fruit and my preference is for fish, blood and bone, which is an organically based mixture. An alternative would be an artificial mixture, such as Growmore. But this general fertilizer is ideally supplemented by potassium sulphate (often called sulphate of potash) for the best soft fruit production. A liquid fertilizer, such as the type sold for tomatoes, will similarly supply a high dose of potash. If you have chalky soil in your garden, a proprietary product containing sequestered iron will be useful, especially for raspberries and strawberries which are highly prone to iron deficiency on alkaline soils. There may also be occasions, such as if a plant has been neglected, when a boost of nitrogen is much needed and dried blood or ammonium sulphate (sulphate of amonia) will provide this.

SUPPLEMENTARY WATERING

As I've already mentioned, water is very important to soft fruit plants and mulching with organic matter on already damp soil in both the autumn and the spring will help to maintain the soil moisture in a fairly uniform state. Even so, during very dry periods, supplementary water may be needed particularly at the

---

MULCHING

I've made references in a number of places throughout this book to mulching, but it is a technique that still engenders a wariness. I think this stems from a disbelief that several centimetres of compost or other organic matter laid on the soil surface won't be positively harmful to the plants. Be assured that it won't. I routinely lay 10-15cm (4-6in) of compost on my light soil around the base of soft fruit canes and bushes twice a year, in spring and autumn. It serves its purpose of moisture retention and weed suppression but within three or four months (even less in a hot summer), it has vanished; dragged into the soil by worms, oxidized into carbon dioxide or used by plants as a source (admittedly a modest source) of nutrients.

Mulching as a weed suppressant achieves its effect by denying the weeds the light that they need to thrive. Whilst the shoots of a deep-rooted perennial will still have the energy to force its way upwards, the tiny food reserves available to an annual weed seedling mean that it will die of starvation long before it is able to grow through a mulch to reach the light.

An alternative mulching method that has found some favour in recent years is black plastic sheeting. This obviously denies light to weeds and limits water loss from the soil surface. But of course it plays no part in the improvement of soil structure and to my mind, looks frightful. Having a fruit garden that is aesthetically pleasing is only slightly lower in my order of priorities than having one that crops well.

time the fruit are beginning to swell. It can either be supplied by a watering can or more efficiently (and if permitted) by a sprinkler or a trickle irrigation system. But don't waste water; do limit it to the period when the fruit need it, when they are filling out, and don't apply it wastefully between the plants rather than where it is needed – which is around their bases.

SPRINKLERS

When water usage isn't legally restricted during drought periods, a sprinkler offers the best method of supplying supplementary irrigation to your soft fruit garden. But do choose a sprinkler that offers the best coverage for your purpose - far too many gardeners use sprinklers that give a circular pattern of spread to water a rectangular area. In consequence, some parts are missed altogether while water is thrown wastefully over neighbouring paths or perhaps even over the wall onto someone else's patio! Do measure the area that you wish to irrigate and then check carefully the pattern of spread before buying a sprinkler.

Rows of commercially grown strawberries being watered by a sprinkler system, which will be evenly rotated

PRUNING AND TRAINING

Although you can produce fruit crops without pruning (wild plants, after all, manage tolerably well), there's no doubt that an unpruned plant will soon become a tangle of growth, its cropping efficiency will decline and it will look far less attractive.

Pruning a mature blackcurrant bush in mid-winter

Pruning isn't complicated, although the individual requirements of different types of soft fruit vary considerably: autumn-fruiting primocane raspberries, for example, should simply be cut completely to soil level in the early part of the year, whereas an established cordon-trained gooseberry must have its side-shoots shortened twice a season. I've given full information under the individual entries, but there is an underlying principle and logic to all of it.

PRUNING SYSTEMS

The essence of pruning a fruit plant is to remove parts either that have passed their time of peak contribution to the plant's fruiting efficiency, or that will never play a useful part in promoting it. Left on the plant, they will divert valuable food and water resources away from the fruit and then, in time, as they become moribund, serve to encourage the establishment of pests and diseases. The main reason that different pruning systems are used for different types of plant is that their flowers and, subsequently, their fruit are borne in varying ways. The primocane raspberry is the extreme example of a plant that bears its flowers on shoots produced during the current year. It is precisely because it takes until the

Cutting out spindly shoots whilst the fruit is still hanging on the bush

end of the season for them to have sufficient time to mature that they *are* autumn- and not summer-fruiting. But the old fruited canes do afford a small degree of frost protection during the winter, so don't cut them out straightaway, but wait until the late winter or early spring when you should then prune them all right down to soil level.

By contrast, a grapevine also bears its flowers and fruits on the current season's shoots, but with the significant difference that these shoots are themselves borne on an established older woody framework. Thus, whilst the fruited shoots are also cut out completely in late winter, they are cut, not back to soil level but back to the junction with the main stem, or rod as it is called.

There are other variations: for example, blackcurrants bear the most abundant fruit on one-year-old wood with some on two- and three-year-old wood but little on wood older than that. By contrast, red and white currants and gooseberries fruit on short spurs borne on old wood. In all instances, the pruning suggested takes account of these different fruiting habits. See pruning advice under individual entries.

Where there is a choice of shoots

to cut out, always cut the oldest or the most misplaced first. The oldest will generally be thicker and tougher; and by misplaced, I mean such examples as blackcurrant branches that hang below the horizontal and would, therefore, be dragged to the soil with the weight of fruit, or raspberry canes that arise 30cm (12in) or more from the main row.

TOOLS FOR PRUNING

You won't prune neatly and well without suitable tools. For soft fruit canes and bushes, two should suffice: secateurs and loppers. Because you will be pruning very few soft young shoots (and even these are generally better nipped out with finger and thumb) but a great deal of harder, woodier stems, single-bladed anvil pattern secateurs are better than the scissor or by-pass type. And anvil-style long-handled loppers will enable you to cut through thicker branches – old blackcurrant stems that need

to be cut out at soil level, for instance. As a general rule, even with the largest model of anvil secateurs, you shouldn't try cutting stems thicker than approximately 2cm (¾in), whereas most good loppers will deal with stems up to about 3.2cm (1¼in) thick.

TRAINING PLANTS

I like to think of training as a means of keeping a plant in a neat and manageable state so that its pruning can be performed satisfactorily. Indeed, in the early stages, the pruning itself is often described as 'formative' and is done with the purpose of training a plant for the long-term. Strictly, training means persuading a plant to grow in a way and direction that is of your choosing.

SUPPORT FOR PLANTS

Many types of soft fruit must be trained against some form of support, for their stems are too weak to support themselves properly when free-standing. The climbing fruits, grapes and Kiwi fruits are the obvious examples of this but the pliable-caned blackberries and their relatives would also be reduced to a mound of tangled growth such as those produced by their wild version, the bramble, if wires were not used to support them. And while wild raspberries are short, rather stiff-stemmed plants, most of the cultivated varieties have tall, rather flexible canes that are easily damaged by strong winds.

By and large, the bush fruits (currants and gooseberries) need no physical support when grown in the conventional manner. But they can very usefully be trained in cordon

form, where one or more vertical shoots are persuaded to grow vertically, the remainder being cut out. And in this form, the single tall shoot will, indeed, be unstable unless it is tied to canes and wires. I've dealt at some length with the way to construct wire support systems in my account of raspberry growing.

But while a free-standing bush needs no support, it still requires some training if it is to be cropped efficiently. Some of the shoots must be cut out at an early stage to prevent overcrowding and those that remain should be chosen carefully to produce a goblet-shaped plant with a fairly hollow central area. The effort needed is relatively little but a well and carefully trained bush will crop more effectively through being easier to prune and manage. And to my eye at least, a well trained soft fruit garden will always be so much more pleasing to look at and work in.

Ideally supported raspberry canes

Gooseberry pruning requires care

PROPAGATION

Unusually for a gardening book, the propagation section here is short. This is not because I would, in any way, wish to dissuade gardeners from propagating their own plants in general; it is because of the reasons that I have outlined on p.16: fruit plants, by and large, must be multiplied vegetatively in order to maintain the purity of the varieties; and any soft fruit plant regularly propagated in this way will progressively become contaminated with virus.

Strawberry plants clearly showing stolon runners

It is wise to purchase Kiwi fruit direct from a quality nursery

If your canes and bushes are vigorous, apparently healthy and yielding well, you are, of course, perfectly at liberty to take cuttings (or pot-up runners in the case of strawberries). But if you already have healthy plants, there would seem to be little point in renewing the stock in any event. Nonetheless, should there be circumstances when, in spite of my warnings, you do wish to propagate your own stock, there are different ways in which this can be done.

CANE FRUITS

Raspberries are multiplied by removing already rooted suckers and replanting them. Blackberries and other pliable cane fruits may be multiplied as hardwood cuttings but can be tip-layered. The tips of low hanging canes will often self-layer but if a shoot tip must be pegged down into a small hole in late-summer, rooting will take about nine months.

GOOSEBERRIES

Most bush fruits are easily propagated by hardwood cuttings, but gooseberries are something of an exception to this, in that they are intrinsically difficult to root because of their very hard wood. Fortunately, however, they also tend to be comparatively long-lived, and are less prone to viral contamination than most bush fruits, so the need for propagation arises relatively infrequently. Blueberries are also extremely difficult to strike from cuttings and their propagation really is a job for an experienced nurseryman.

Having cut the 'vine eyes', push them into compost and place in a propagator

Established vines such as these take many years to grow, but patience is rewarded with succulent and tasty fruit

HARDWOOD CUTTINGS

Hardwood cuttings are best taken in the early winter, before all the leaves have fallen, using sections of the current year's shoots about 20cm (8in) long and with the tip portion of softer wood trimmed off. Remove any persisting leaves and bury the shoots for about three-quarters of their length in a narrow slit-style trench in a sheltered part of the garden. Ideally, a little sand and bone meal mixture should be sprinkled in the bottom of the trench and the cuttings then firmed in. They should root within about 12 months.

It's unlikely that most gardeners will want to propagate their own grapevines and Kiwi fruit, although it is relatively easy to do. Hardwood cuttings may be taken as I've described above, but a more convenient technique for grapes is in early spring, by using very short pieces of stem called 'vine eyes', each about 2cm (1in) long and each bearing a bud. Push the 'vine eye' cuttings into a 3:1 mixture of sand and soil-based potting compost so the bud just protrudes. Place the cuttings in a warm propagator.

PROPAGATING STRAWBERRIES

Strawberries produce stolons bearing small plantlets; both the stolon and the plantlets themselves are referred to as runners. Normally, these should be removed so the plants direct their energy into fruit production but if they are needed to multiply the stock, they can be left in place. After six to eight weeks, they will have rooted sufficiently for them to be transplanted.

FRUIT CAGES AND PLANT PROTECTION

I can't honestly say that soft fruit are uniquely attractive to birds but they are certainly high on the list of garden plants that suffer most from bird damage. I know that some vegetables are commonly damaged by pigeons, while fruit trees, and pears especially, seem extraordinarily appealing to bullfinches. But birds of many types find soft fruit plants worthy of their attention at most times of the year. The fruit are clearly desirable to them as food in the summer, although they do tend to ripen at a time when there is plenty of other food material available. Most gardeners find that it is during the winter months that birds cause the greatest damage by feeding on the buds, and it's in the cold months, with food supplies in general fairly low, that a fruit cage really pays for itself.

A sturdy and robust fruit cage offers excellent protection for soft fruit

Ripe raspberries - well protected!

PROTECTIVE CAGES

I know that I share many other gardeners' sentiments in saying that I simply couldn't grow soft fruit without proper protection. At a pinch, canes and bushes can be protected by throwing loose netting over them, but this is rarely very satisfactory and I have to say that my own considerable investment in plants and time would be wasted without the added cost of a decent cage. There are now several proprietary fruit cages available in fairly readily assembled kit form. Most comprise a light tubular aluminium frame over which light-weight plastic netting is fitted.

Modern modular construction means that almost any size of cage can be constructed to fit your own range of plants. Alternatively, a more robust cage can be made from rustic poles of treated timber but whatever method is used, a fruit cage should be no less than 2m (6ft) tall.

NETTING

The netting should be chosen carefully and be of a mesh size that will exclude small birds and yet be unlikely to trap their legs. The ideal mesh is between about 1.3cm (½in) and 2cm (¾in) across. The side netting on proprietary fruit cages is usually plastic but galvanised chicken wire makes a stronger construction for cages with wooden frames. Galvanized wire should not be used for the top netting, however. Not only is it harder to support than lightweight plastic, but damage to fruit plants will occur from zinc, washed from the netting by rain. Lower cages of similar style, about 30cm (12in) tall (and with no door) can be used for strawberry beds, although growing early strawberries under cloches obviates the need for any additional protection.

SEASONAL CROPPING

Achieving a balance between glut and scarcity (or, in historical times, between feast and famine) is a problem for anyone who grows food plants. In our gardens, it is, of course, more of an inconvenience than a disaster if all of the strawberries and raspberries ripen in the same week; but it is annoying nonetheless.

PLANNING FOR CONTINUITY

Fortunately, there is a way around the problem. Individually, soft fruit plants are fairly small; even a blackcurrant bush is a modest thing compared with a plum tree. You will, therefore, almost invariably grow more than one plant of each type of fruit (a great many more in the case of strawberries). By ensuring that your plants include at least two and ideally more varieties with different maturing times, you will be able to have continuity of cropping.

CROPPING TIME

Under each variety description, I have indicated if it is early, mid-season or late-maturing, although I have resisted trying to relate these times to calendar months because the season overall will vary by up to two or more weeks from region to region. Apart from strawberries (where complications such as longevity of the plants are involved), raspberries offer a much greater range of varieties than any other soft fruit – a reflection of their high commercial importance. On p.44, therefore, I have suggested a selection of summer-fruiting varieties to achieve a

Early white currants growing next to mid-season red currants - an example of how you can make use of different varieties' cropping times

fairly continuous cropping pattern over the two months or so of the fruiting season.

Almost without exception, soft fruit are self-fertile and there is thus no need, as there is with many tree fruit, to ensure that you have compatible varieties able to cross-pollinate each other. If space in your fruit garden is limited, however, then choose a range of several varieties that ripen sequentially for those types of soft fruit (like raspberries) that remain fresh for a very short time on the plant, and have a single variety of those (such as gooseberries) for which the cropping season overall is short or one on which the fruit will hang on the plant for a reasonably long period.

PICKING AND PRESERVING

Once soft fruit has been picked, it tends to deteriorate quickly. If you are not going to eat it straightaway, the best alternative is to preserve it.

Logic suggests that fruit should not be picked until it is ripe, and with most this is true, although Kiwi fruit and to some extent strawberries can be picked when slightly immature to prolong their keeping period. But it's because the period of optimum ripeness is often rather short before the fruit deteriorates, that choosing a range of varieties for sequential cropping makes sound sense. In the notes for each fruit type, I've suggested when and how they should be picked as this isn't always obvious. Confronted with Kiwi fruit for the first time, for instance, people are uncertain whether to use scissors, fingers or secateurs. And while gooseberries are cut individually with scissors, blackcurrants are best picked by hand in bunches. But must strawberries be fully red before they are picked? And how many gardeners have wondered if loganberries can be ripe when it's impossible to separate the fruit from the core?

Picking strigs of blackcurrants by hand as they ripen

JAM-MAKING

Once picked, soft fruit will fairly soon moulder; only the Kiwi fruit remains firm and palatable for more than a week or so. For as long as they have been grown however, soft fruit have been preserved in some way and although I confess to not knowing when strawberry jam was invented, I suspect it has been with us for a very long time. The value of fruit for jam making and similar types

of preserving is largely related to their pectin content which dictates the consistency of the finished product. This declines as the fruit softens with ripeness so they are better picked, for this purpose, slightly under- rather than slightly over-ripe. But pectin content does vary with each variety and I have, therefore, indicated in every chapter, where specific varieties are especially good for making into jam.

JELLIES, BUTTERS, CHEESES

Other traditional types of preserving which are also possible include jellies; red currant and blackcurrant being the most popular ones today. And there are also fruit butters and cheeses, which are made using puréed fruit and contain slightly less sugar than jams. If stored in properly sterilized jars, they should all remain palatable for some time.

OTHER METHODS OF PRESERVING

Other techniques are possible with particular types of fruit and have been used extensively in the past. Juice production, and its obvious consequence wine making, are familiar enough, especially with grapes, but grapes, probably alone among soft fruit, can also be preserved by the oldest method of all, drying. Sauces, pickles and chutneys can be made with soft fruit, either alone or in combination with other types of fruit or vegetable. But until recently, there has been only one method of preserving that maintained the fruit in something approaching its original shape, texture and flavour, and that was bottling. The principle is easy enough to understand for it simply comprises packing the fruit in a glass jar, covering it with a syrup or similar liquid and then heating the whole to a high temperature to sterilize it before sealing. Almost all types of soft fruit can be bottled with varying success and it is equally effective with all varieties. As a devotee of bottled produce, I can personally only lament its gradual fall from favour in the face of competition from *the* food preserving technique of modern times, home freezing.

FREEZING

All types of soft fruit can be frozen but some are a great deal more successful than others, mainly because they maintain their texture and shape better. Strawberries are difficult to freeze well and, I think, are really only satisfactory when they are to be re-used for cooking afterwards. There are several methods of freezing – in sugar, dry frozen with no additives, in a syrup, as a purée or pre-poached being the commonest. By and large, dry freezing and sugar freezing are the best methods to use for soft fruit and, again, I have indicated in the individual entries which varieties are particularly suitable for preserving by freezing. But whichever method is used, do be sure to use only the very best, blemish-free fruit at the absolute peak of ripeness; and try to pick sequentially in batches so that the fruit are frozen as soon as possible after picking.

Fruits of your labour - delicious homemade jam

A QUICK METHOD OF BOTTLING FRUIT

Granulated sugar
Lemon juice
1kg (2.2lb) bottling jars with lids
Large saucepan, big enough to hold the jars with a close fitting lid
Fruit (raspberries, blackberries, hybrid berries, blackcurrants, gooseberries, red and white currants, blueberries or cranberries)

Prepare syrup by adding 450g (1lb) sugar to ½litre (17fl oz) water, bring slowly to the boil, stir continuously and boil for two minutes. Add a further ½litre (17fl oz) water and two dessert spoonfuls of lemon juice.

Remove all the stalks from the fruit. Ensure that the jars are scrupulously clean, rinse in warm water and allow to drain briefly. Carefully fill the jars with the fruit, using a wooden spatula to pack them but take care not to crush any. Fill the jars to the brim and then pour the prepared hot syrup over them, filling to the top. Shake the jars gently to remove any air bubbles. While the jars are still hot, seal them and then place them in the pan with small pieces of cloth between each to prevent cracking.

Add hot water up to the level of the liquid within the jars and heat very slowly so that simmering temperature 88°C (190°F) is attained in about 30 minutes. Simmer for two minutes and then allow the jars to cool for 24 hours. Carefully remove the sealing clip or band and hold each jar by its lid to ensure that a vacuum has formed before replacing the seal and storing the jars.

CONTAINERS

There are very few garden plants that can't be grown in containers although I have to say that soft fruit don't make particularly successful subjects. This is largely because most types are fairly shallowly rooted and, therefore, prone to drying out. Any plant in a container will suffer more easily from water shortage than one in the open garden; and water shortage in a fruiting plant means poor quality fruit. All of these factors can lead to problems, but if you are prepared to devote more than the normal amount of attention to watering and plant initially with care, then it is possible to obtain modest crops of soft fruit, even on a paved area by someone with no real garden.

A row of grapevines establishing well in plastic containers

TYPES OF CONTAINERS

Because of their small size, strawberries are the most amenable of soft fruit to container cultivation and I have discussed this in some detail on p.91. For all other types of soft fruit, a container approximately of half-barrel size is needed – around 50cm (20in) in both height and diameter. Genuine wooden half barrels are suitable provided drainage holes are made in the bottom and the inside is lined with plastic sheeting to prolong the life of the timber. Alternatively, use terracotta, if you can afford the high cost of large pots. Plastic containers will suffice, however they will never look as attractive and are quite likely to crack and split after a few years.

It is very important to use a good quality growing medium and for these long-term crops, a soil-based type such as John Innes No. 3 potting compost is ideal. The only exception to this are blueberries which must have a highly acid medium and can only be grown in ericaceous compost of the type sold for growing rhododendrons and camellias. Although soil-based composts are well furnished initially with nutrients, regular feeding will be necessary after the first six months or so and my general advice is to follow the fertilizer regimes that I have

Strawberries in a terracotta pot

One of the most interesting developments in container raising of soft fruit in recent years has been to grow strawberries in long containers above head height in greenhouses so the fruit hangs down, for ease of picking. Commercially, various systems have been adopted, including the use of growing bags of soilless compost and wide diameter sections of plastic gutter pipe into which drainage holes have been drilled. Of course, any system of this type does depend on having strong shelves to support the containers and, ideally, on installing some system of automated irrigation and provision of liquid feed. I don't think it is a technique for every garden but a gardener with a large, more or less redundant greenhouse could make excellent use of the facility and could extend the strawberry cropping season considerably by using any of my recommended day-neutral varieties (see p.97). These will crop all year round if temperatures are adequate as they aren't dependent, like the more familiar and older varieties, on the long days of summer for flowering to commence.

outlined under each plant entry for normal outdoor growing but supplement this with liquid feeding. Apply a proprietary tomato fertilizer or similar product with a high potash content about once every two weeks.

REGULAR WATERING

I've already mentioned the importance of regular watering, especially when the fruit are beginning to form but don't forget to apply a thick mulch too. Pulverised bark is a good choice and also an attractive one and should be applied when the compost is damp – once in the spring and again in the autumn.

GENERAL MAINTENANCE

Pruning and pest and disease control should be done exactly as if the plants were growing in the open soil but you should be prepared for slightly more pest and disease problems if, as is generally the case, the container is positioned in a relatively sheltered spot.

It is unusual to see a blueberry bush growing in a container, but it can be done as long as ericaceous compost is used and the plant is well mulched

PESTS AND DISEASES

I've already mentioned the importance of viruses (and the even greater importance of avoiding them) in soft fruit growing, but as a group, these plants are prone to a considerable number of other problems, too. Because the types of pest and diseases vary somewhat between the different types of fruit plant, I've given more specific details in table form under the individual chapters but there are some general principles about pests and diseases that are more appropriately dealt with here.

Rust on a blackberry stem

Diseases in plants are caused by viruses, by fungi or by bacteria, although bacterial problems are relatively insignificant in soft fruit. The importance of viruses stems from the fact that they are total parasites – they are unable to live and multiply away from the tissues of their hosts. And being totally dependent on the host means that they impose a major drain on its resources. Once a virus is present within the tissues, the plant gradually, almost imperceptibly, declines in vigour and fruit production. Although there can be obviously misshapen leaves with mottling or other patterns, virus contamination may not be revealed at all until the cropping is impaired.

FUNGAL DISEASES

Diseases caused by fungi are much less insidious and the two most important types on soft fruit are powdery mildews and botrytis grey mould, which may attack both the fruit, causing decay and the stems, causing a dieback. By and large, different types of mildew affect different types of plant so the commonest species on gooseberries, American mildew, won't transfer to raspberries, although it will affect currants which are more closely related. The most important pests on soft fruit are aphids, different species of which attack all types of plant. Apart from their role in bringing virus contamination, their sap-sucking activities can seriously weaken plants too.

It's an old adage in gardening that avoidance is better than control. And avoidance of pest and disease problems is best achieved by selecting varieties that are resistant to attack. Unfortunately, while resistance has been a major goal of plant breeders for many years, we still have relatively few soft fruit varieties for which it offers a complete answer although I have, of course, referred to these where appropriate. Among some of the greatest successes are aphid-resistant raspberries and mildew-resistant gooseberries.

VIRUS-FREE PLANTS

Viruses are a special case, however, because initial avoidance is possible through the use of virus-free plants

Blister damage to a red currant leaf caused by aphid attack

BIOLOGICAL CONTROL

Sadly, though a number of biological control systems are fairly effective in greenhouses, most notably for greenfly and whitefly control, their value in the outdoor fruit garden is almost nil. Interestingly however, two recent developments may offer some hope for the future. A biological control for vine weevil is now available and may be useful in established strawberry beds where the pest is troublesome, while a biological control for slugs is not far from final development. Both use species of predatory eelworm as the controlling agents.

(p.16) but even these won't stay virus-free forever because virus-carrying aphids and, sometimes, eelworms in the soil, will gradually introduce them into the plants with their feeding activities. Clearly, the only way that this can be minimized is by paying careful attention to aphid control, but it's an inescapable fact that soft fruit plants must be replaced fairly regularly. Strawberries will be renewed frequently in any event, but among the longer term conventional soft fruit crops, only gooseberries are relatively free from virus problems and may, therefore, crop for twenty or more years.

Although the impact of diseases can be lessened by good husbandry – not overcrowding the plants and not overfeeding them with nitrogen for example – you will probably be faced from time to time with the need for a fungicide spray. Most soft fruit diseases, and certainly mildew

and grey mould, can be controlled with the organically acceptable sulphur, or with a synthetic systemic fungicide such as benomyl, thiophanate-methyl or carbendazim. Care should be taken when using sulphur on gooseberries, however, as some varieties are damaged by it and are said to be sulphur-shy. 'Careless' and 'Leveller' are the commonest of those still widely grown on which sulphur shouldn't be used. Red and white currants can also be damaged by sulphur under some circumstances, for example, such as during very hot weather.

APHID CONTROL

Because of their twin-pronged nuisance value as virus vectors and sap suckers, aphids really must be controlled and although I would like to be able to say that encouraging beneficial, predator insects into the fruit garden by planting flowers nearby will do the job, I can't be totally enthusiastic. Nonetheless, such well

Effects of American mildew on a gooseberry fruit

known insect attractants as marigolds and herbs will look extremely pretty when planted around the fruit garden and will certainly help with the cause.

When choosing an insecticide for aphid control, I try to limit myself to three very different ones. In the winter, when the plants are dormant, I always apply a tar oil spray to the bare stems. This is invaluable in killing the overwintering eggs and adults on the bark. But with the best of wills, this may not be the complete answer and a contact spray will also be needed at the first signs of attack in the summer. Then, I use either a soap-based spray, applying it in the evening, when harmless and beneficial insects are least likely to be affected, or a product containing the synthetic pesticide pirimicarb which is largely specific, in its action, to aphids.

OTHER PESTS

Of course, other insect pests will occur from time to time but similar treatments may be used against them. The biggest difficulties arise with non-insect pests, mites especially. Big bud mites on blackcurrants are considered on p.68 but red spider mites are a real annoyance too. In common with other mites, they are little affected by insecticides and tend to thrive in hot, dry conditions. Ensuring that the plants are well mulched and not allowed to dry out will help to create an environment in which red spider mites are discouraged but if individual plants become consistently and severely affected, it might be sensible to destroy them and begin again with fresh stock of a different variety.

MONTH BY MONTH CARE

Inspect soft fruit regularly for symptoms of pests and diseases. Refer to main entries for specific diagnosis and treatment.

MID-WINTER

■ Mail-order bare-rooted plants continue to arrive. They must be planted promptly or heeled in. Container-grown plants can be dealt with when convenient.

■ Continue planting raspberries. They produce their best crops in full sun, and should ideally be planted in rows running north-south. Add bone meal to the planting trench. Water well, mulch and cut back to just above a bud, about 25cm (10in) above soil level.

■ Plant two-year-old, container-grown blueberries, and other acid-soil fruits in acid, humus-rich soil or in containers of ericaceous compost.

■ Most established soft fruit should now be fed with sulphate of potash at a rate of 34g per square metre (1oz per square yard). This is suitable for raspberries, blackcurrants, blackberries and hybrid berries, gooseberries, red and white currants.

■ This is the last chance to apply a tar oil winter wash to dormant fruit canes and bushes.

LATE WINTER

■ Raspberry planting should be completed as soon as possible. Established primocane raspberries can be cut to soil level. New canes will appear in a few weeks.

■ Formative and regular pruning of gooseberries, and red and white currants can be carried out now.

■ Cut out the fruited shoots of well-established grapevines to the junc-

On a chill frosty morning, the soft fruit bushes lie dormant

tion with the rod.

■ Grapes can be propagated by taking 'vine eyes' - 2cm-(¾in-)long pieces of stem including a bud. These are pushed into a mixture of 3:1 sand and soil-based potting medium and placed in a heated propagator.

■ Check for the symptoms of big bud mite on blackcurrants - remove and burn any affected shoots, then spray with benomyl.

EARLY SPRING

■ Feed grapevines using general fertilizer, such as Growmore or fish, blood and bone at a rate of 34g per square metre (1oz per square yard).

■ The same regime is suitable for most soft fruit, including Kiwi fruit,

raspberries, blackberries and hybrid berries, blackcurrants and gooseberries. Follow by a mulch of well rotted compost.

■ Symptoms of iron deficiency, to which raspberries are particularly prone, can be remedied by applying sequestered iron, following the manufacturer's recommendations.

■ Feed blueberries with sulphate of potash and sulphate of ammonia, both at a rate of 17g per square metre (½oz per square yard). Mulch with coniferous sawdust. Also mulch cranberries with lime-free sand, and water with collected rainwater.

■ Feed strawberries with sulphate of potash at a rate of 17g per square metre (½oz per square yard). For an early crop of strawberries, cover established plants with cloches.

■ Alpine strawberry seeds can be sown now.

MID-SPRING

■ Cape gooseberries, raised from seed in warmth, can be planted out in 20cm (8in) pots of soil-based compost in a greenhouse, with a minimum temperature of about 7°C (45° F).

■ Sow melon seeds on edge, at 21°C (70°F), in soil-based sowing compost, grow on until they have four true leaves, then plant in enriched greenhouse borders, or harden off for at least 10 days before planting out in a cold frame or cloche.

■ Plant Kiwi fruit in a sheltered position. Male and female plants will be needed for pollination. Do not allow established plants to dry out.

■ Strawberries can be planted from now until late summer to crop the following year. Prepare the planting site a week ahead with Growmore or fish, blood and bone at a rate of 68g per square metre (2oz per square yard), and rake in.

■ Strawberries under cloches need ventilation on sunny days.

LATE SPRING

■ Prepare outdoor beds for Cape gooseberries by raking in a general fertilizer about a week before planting. The plants, raised from seed in

warmth, can be planted in a sheltered position once all risk of frost is past. Tie in carefully, and feed when the first fruit has set.

■ Tie in melon shoots, training and pinching out as described on p.105-106. The flowers must be pollinated by hand, use a soft brush.

■ The first protected strawberries are ready to pick. As fruitlets form on outdoor plants, place either straw, bracken or strawberry mats underneath to lift them slightly off the soil.

■ Keep a watch for aphids, and spray before they really become a problem, using a soap-based spray in the evening, when there should be no pollinating insects present, or a synthetic insecticide such as pirimicarb, which is almost entirely specific to aphids.

■ Keep a watch for caterpillars and spray with a contact insecticide or remove them by hand, using gloves, if you can bear to.

EARLY SUMMER

■ Feed melons once a week when the fruit begin to swell, using liquid fertilizer with a high potash content. Sudden wilting may occur if the plants have been grown for several years in the same greenhouse bed.

■ Water grapevines generously all summer, and apply a liquid feed with a high potash content every couple of weeks. Dessert grapes are thinned out using round-ended scissors, so the individual fruits have room to swell. Look out for mildew and botrytis, particularly on greenhouse vines.

■ Established Kiwi fruit are coming into flower. Even with male and

Early spring growth showing on the old canes and at the base of the plants

MONTH BY MONTH CARE

female plants present, fruit set will be improved if you help nature along by transferring pollen from the male to female flowers with a soft brush. Do not allow the plants to dry out at this stage.

■ Perennial weeds among raspberries are best dealt with using a weedkiller containing glyphosate, as hoeing will damage the shallow roots.

■ Fruit grown in containers will need extra feeding. Apply a liquid tomato or similar potash-rich feed every two weeks.

■ Runners are forming on established strawberry plants but propagating from them entails the risk of spreading disease.

MID-SUMMER

■ Pick ripe fruit regularly. Tie in fast-growing canes.

■ Water regularly in dry periods, preferably not in the heat of the day, when drips on leaves could cause scorching and most of the water will evaporate very quickly.

■ Fungus diseases are common at this time of year. Mildew and botrytis grey mould can be controlled with sulphur or a systemic fungicide, such as benomyl, thiophanate-methyl or carbendazim. Some types of fruit can be damaged by sulphur (see p.31).

■ Keep a look out for the symptoms of virus, and continue to control aphids which can transmit them. If

symptoms are severe, there is no alternative but to uproot and destroy affected plants by burning them completely. Never try to propagate from plants showing signs of virus. Replant on a fresh site if possible, and use only certified stock.

■ Hot dry conditions favour red spider mite, particularly under glass. Chemical control is almost impossible, but they dislike damp conditions, so you could try misting plants with water. If all else fails, you may have to destroy the plants and start again with a new variety.

LATE SUMMER

■ As summer-fruiting raspberries are picked, cut out the spent fruited canes and start to tie in new ones, choosing the best placed. Hoe or pull out those that are not required.

■ Pliable canes, such as those of blackberries, can be tip-layered, by pegging a shoot tip down into a shallow hole. Rooting should occur within nine months.

■ Gooseberries and red and white currants can be given their summer pruning about now, preferably about six weeks after midsummer.

■ Cut back foliage of perennial strawberries once the last fruit have been picked. If the crop has been disappointing, feed with sulphate of potash at a rate of 17g per square metre (½oz per square yard).

EARLY AUTUMN

■ Clear up fallen leaves regularly. They can harbour pests and fungal spores.

■ Plant Kiwi fruit now to give the plants a chance of establishing before winter. In particularly cold areas delay until mid-spring. Harvest fruit

At the height of summer, ripe fruit needs picking regularly

from established plants before the first frosts. They will continue to ripen indoors.

■ Prune blackberries and hybrid berries by cutting off the old canes at soil level once they have fruited. New canes can then be retrained in their place, according to the method you are following.

■ Blackcurrants can be pruned from fruit maturity until mid-winter. If done now, the fruit can be harvested from the cut branches. Blueberries are pruned in the same way. Each year cut between a quarter and a third of all shoots back to just above ground level, starting with the oldest. This ensures a regular supply of new shoots.

■ A new fruit garden can be planned and prepared during autumn. Order bare-rooted plants from specialist nurseries once you have decided on the varieties you want.

MID-AUTUMN

■ Apply an organic mulch around bushes and canes when the soil is damp to help retain moisture and protect the roots against the frosts and cold of winter.

■ Autumn cultivation can be carried out for new fruit gardens. Thorough digging, removing perennial weeds, correcting drainage, and incorporating plenty of well rotted organic matter should all be completed before the first plants arrive in early winter. Construct support structures and fruit cages while the ground is soft enough to drive in stakes.

LATE AUTUMN

■ Make sure that fruit cages and nets are in good repair. In winter, when food supplies are running low,

A few autumn-fruiting raspberries are still left on the canes

birds may resort to stripping your fruit bushes of buds.

■ Cut down perennial Cape gooseberries grown in the greenhouse. Seeds for greenhouse plants can be sown at this time of year.

■ Complete pruning of blackberries and hybrid berries

EARLY WINTER

■ Apply tar oil winter wash to dormant plants to control aphids and other overwintering pests.

■ Inspect your fruit garden regularly. Check ties and supports after high winds and make repairs as necessary. Cut out obviously damaged shoots immediately.

■ Take hardwood cuttings of sound,

healthy plants before all the leaves have fallen. They should form roots within a year.

■ Bare-rooted raspberries, blackberries, hybrid berries, and red and white currants establish well if planted in winter - either now or, if the soil is frozen or waterlogged, during the next couple of months. Blackcurrants and gooseberries, however, should be planted before mid-winter, as they start into growth relatively early.

■ Grapevines are best planted at this time, when fully dormant. Add plenty of well-rotted organic matter to the planting hole, and a light dressing of bone meal.

RASPBERRIES

" Raspberries have so much going for them: because of their upright habit, they produce a relatively large crop from a very small area of ground; they are simplicity itself to prune; and by choosing your varieties carefully, it's possible to have fresh fruit for a period of at least 4 months. Most varieties freeze well without disintegrating and so, of all soft fruit, the raspberry probably comes closest to being available in more or less the same, recognizable form all year round. Apart from having rather stiff instead of flexible canes, they differ principally (and most usefully) from related species of Rubus, *such as the blackberry, in that the ripe fruit separates easily from the plug or receptacle when they are picked. "*

HISTORY AND TYPES OF RASPBERRY

The value of the raspberry has been appreciated since ancient times although for many centuries it was the fruit of the wild *Rubus idaeus* that was collected. But at first it seems they were gathered more for medicinal than food use. *Rubus idaeus* grows in many parts of the world, usually in woodland habitats but by the sixteenth century, in England at least, it was being planted in gardens. Although its fruits can be sweet and delicious, they are small compared with those of the cultivated raspberries that we know today. It's a very variable species, however, and gradually larger-fruited forms were selected for garden cultivation and

gradually, too, both red- and yellow-coloured types became available to European gardeners. The so-called yellows range, in practice, from a rich gold to an extremely pale yellow-fruited variant that was known historically as the white raspberry. There are also black-fruited species and varieties and even purples too, produced by crossing the red with the black. Black raspberries are less hardy than red, however, and have never been as popular in Europe as in North America where they originated. In the present century, a good deal of research has been devoted to producing new and better raspberry varieties, especially those with disease resistance. The North American raspberry species *Rubus strigosus* and several others too have been used in making the crosses.

Apart from fruit colour, modern garden raspberries are divided into two main groups depending on the

way that the fruit are borne. Most raspberries fruit on the canes produced in the previous season but there is a small group of varieties, called primocane raspberries, that fruit on the tips of the current season's canes. They bear a smaller crop but help in extending the cropping period well into the autumn. The cultivation of the two groups is similar in all respects except for pruning.

SOIL

The classic, fairly deep medium loam with a pH around 6.5 is the ideal raspberry soil. On wet, cold, heavy soils they will grow very inadequately while on very light, free-draining sites they will produce small, dry and tasteless fruits although this is less of a problem in areas with a high rainfall. Both heavy and light soils should, therefore, be improved with organic matter before planting but if the soil is very heavy, and very large quantities of organic matter would be required, it is generally still possible to produce a reasonable crop if this improvement is confined to the area of the trenches in which raspberries are planted, rather than over the whole plot. On even slightly alkaline soils, raspberries will display symptoms of iron deficiency which should be corrected (see p.10).

SITE

As they are naturally plants of lightly shaded woodland, raspberries are tolerant of light shade in gardens, and if the soft fruit garden has a slightly shaded area, they will generally grow better there than other types of soft fruit. Nonetheless, the very best crops will always be obtained in full sun and the rows should, if possible,

Adequate shelter is provided for these raspberrries by the hedge at the back and the belt of trees to the side

A good site for raspberry canes, with plenty of direct sunlight

be orientated north-south to make optimum use of this. Shelter from strong winds is important and in very windy spots, it's sensible to choose shorter, stiffer-caned varieties. Raspberries make a good choice in areas prone to spring frosts, however, for they flower late and usually escape frost damage.

PLANTING

Raspberries are best planted in the winter; early winter is ideal but any time when the soil isn't frozen is suitable. They are, in any event, generally sold bare-rooted during the dormant season and do not establish as satisfactorily (even when obtainable) from container-grown stock planted at other times of the year. Usually, raspberries are grown in rows and I find they are most easily planted in a trench rather than in individual planting holes. Although they produce a mass of fibrous roots close to the surface, they do produce deep roots too and so the trench should be at least 45cm (18in) deep and of similar width with plenty of well rotted manure or compost dug in, and a handful of bone meal added per running metre (yard) of row.

The canes or 'stools' should be planted shallowly, with the upper part of the roots about 5cm (2in) deep on top of the carefully firmed contents of the trench. Any new white cane buds should be just at soil level. Planting deeper than this may discourage the production of new canes. Move the canes slightly as the soil is refilled around them to ensure than no air pockets are left, and then firm the soil carefully with your boot, ensuring that the soil slopes slightly

RASPBERRIES

Ideally spaced canes, allowing plenty of room for vigorous, healthy growth

A stout post and wire support system

away from the canes. Water well, top with a mulch of compost and cut back the canes (if this hasn't already been done by the nursery) to just above a bud about 25cm (10in) above soil level.

SPACING

The spacing of the stools and the distance between adjacent rows depends on the variety (and its vigour) and also on the training system used. For most varieties, the rows should be between 1.2 and 1.5m (4 and 5ft) apart (depending, as much as anything, on the space available) but more vigorous types, especially those with widely arching laterals (see the individual descriptions) are better at a spacing of 1.8m (6ft). Spacing within rows for the most popular training method, the English hedgerow system, is 40cm (16in) but there is much to be said for the Scottish stool system (see p.39–40) where the plants are positioned 70cm (28in) apart.

SUPPORTS AND TRAINING

Like all other cane fruits, raspberries must be supported (although at a pinch, you can manage without support for the shorter-caned black- and purple-fruited and also the autumn-fruiting varieties in non-windy areas). Many support and training systems have been developed in different parts of the world although some are only really relevant to commercial fruit farms. The ones I shall describe here are those that I think are the best for garden use.

The easiest and most straightforward method is with horizontal wires strained between vertical posts. Obviously, any type of stout post can be used but my preference, on the grounds of aesthetics and strength, is for round rustic tannelized wooden posts, sharpened and driven 45 or 60cm (18 or 24in) into the soil (not concreted) to leave a height of about 1.8m (6ft) above ground. For rigidity, the posts should be braced with another diagonal post, driven into the ground and bolted on to the vertical half-way up. Although dependent on the overall size of the fruit garden, a row length of about 3.5m (12ft) between posts is ideal if the wires are not to sag.

Use galvanized or, better, plastic-coated wire of about 10 gauge or 3.15mm (⅛in) diameter, suitable for straining – normal tying wire will snap. It can be twisted two or three times around each post or attached to bolts screwed through each post for pulling taut by hand. Alternatively, straining bolts can be fitted at one end to give a tighter pull, although I have seldom found this much use unless completely rigid support posts are used – wooden posts will always 'give' slightly as they expand and contract and you will be forever having to re-tension the wires. The wires are most usefully positioned at approximately 60cm and 1.2m (24in and 4ft) above soil level, although

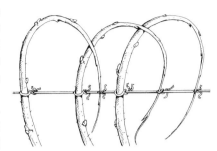

Tie each cane to the support wires in a figure of eight pattern

this spacing isn't critical, and with very tall-growing varieties, three wires may be used, the top one at 1.5m (5ft) or even higher. Individual canes should be tied to the wires with soft degradable garden string (fillis) in a figure of eight pattern or alternatively with a single strand running the length of the wire and wound around it, lacing each cane in turn. It's important to use a biodegradable material as you will have pieces of wire or nylon string forever littering the garden after you have retied the canes each year. Raffia is suitable for individual ties but several strands must be twisted

together to give adequate strength

MAIN TRAINING METHODS

There are two main training methods to choose between for a system of single wires. The English hedgerow system is the most popular and here the crop of canes that emerges from and between each stool is thinned and tied-in to the wires so as to give as uniform and narrow a row as possible, the ideal being to have a cane every 10cm (4in). But although this is the most popular system, I have never found it the easiest, partly because it's difficult to weed between the canes but also because it's well nigh impossible to 'arrange' for them to emerge so uniformly. Much simpler is the Scottish stool system where the canes are allowed to emerge as a group from each stool, excess canes between the stools are cut out, and the canes tied-in, fan-pattern, to the wires.

OTHER TRAINING METHODS

An alternative to the conventional single row is to use a training system that entails having parallel wires. Here, there are three options. The

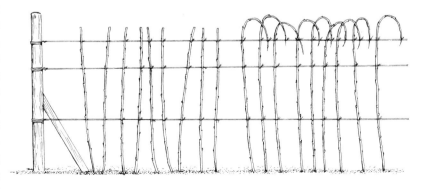

The English hedgerow system

RASPBERRIES

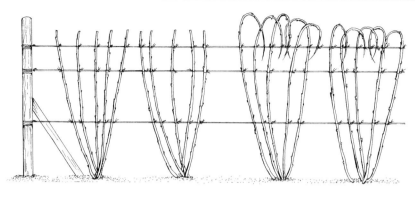

The Scottish stool system

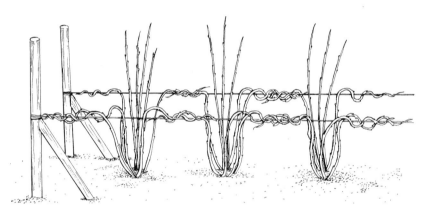

The Scandinavian system

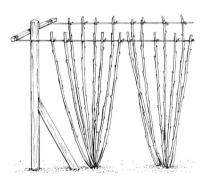

The Worcester system

Worcester system is based on the Scottish stool system but a cross-piece is bolted to the top of each post and one wire run from the end of each. Half of the canes from each stool are then tied to each wire, the principle being to help separate the fruiting canes from the new ones that grow up in the centre. In the other two methods, two complete sets of posts and parallel wires are erected, just like the single wire system but duplicated. In the simplest,

with the wires 60cm (24in) apart, strings are tied across them every 60cm (24in) or so, but the canes are not tied individually, merely confined in groups. There is no fiddly tying-in with this method but it isn't worthwhile using it in windy areas because the canes inevitably suffer damage through being buffeted. It's a system that works well with short-caned autumn fruiting raspberries. Finally, with the two sets of wires 1m (3ft) apart there is the Scandinavian system. Here, there are no cross-strings and the fruiting canes are drawn to the side wires and woven around them, also with the objective of leaving the young canes unharmed in the centre.

If space is very limited, as it can be in small gardens, it is perfectly possible to obtain a small crop of raspberries by planting two stools either side of a single post and tying in four or five canes from each of them. Pruning and all aspects of cultivation are similar to more conventional training methods.

PRUNING AND CANE THINNING

You will have gathered from what I have said about training, that the removal of some canes is an important part of raspberry growing. In practice, this is almost all that there is to raspberry pruning. In the first year after planting, retain and tie-in all the strong, stout canes that grow and simply cut out any feeble ones or any that emerge too far from the stool to enable them to be tied-in.

These canes will fruit in the following season and once the fruit has been picked, they should be cut off

Immediately after planting the raspberries, cut the stumps to 25cm (10in) above ground level

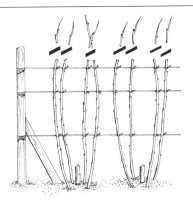

During the spring of all following years, remove the tops to a bud just above the top wire

After fruiting cut the old canes to ground level. Tie the new canes in about 10cm (4in) apart

at soil level and then some of the new canes tied in their place. You can easily recognize the new canes: they are shorter, green with fresh healthy leaves, and of course, no flowers or fruit. But here you must be selective. Again, cut (or better, pull from below soil level) any canes too far from the wires, but you must also cut off excess new canes, even if they are fairly strong ones. With most training systems, try to leave no more than eight or nine canes per metre (yard) of row, whether they are evenly spaced, as in the English hedgerow system or fan-patterned, as in the Scottish stool method. With the Worcester system, retain 18 canes per metre (yard) of row (nine on each wire).

LIMITING SUCKER GROWTH

Raspberry canes, of course, are simply suckers but we tend to use this name only when we don't want them. In good growing conditions, masses of suckers can emerge between the rows and at some considerable distance from them, causing a nuisance in beds and borders. They

Tying down the tops of tall growing raspberry canes (see p.39)

RASPBERRIES

should be hoed or pulled off before they grow more than 15cm (6in) or so tall. You can't prevent sucker growth but it can be limited by burying heavy gauge plastic sheeting vertically to about 75cm (30in) depth, and about a similar distance either side of the row. If previous experience has been that suckers will be a problem, this might be worthwhile when planting a new fruit garden.

EXCESS GROWTH

I've suggested that the top wire on your post and wire system should be about 1.2m (4ft) high. But of course, many raspberry varieties will grow taller than this, and some a very great deal taller, although these are best avoided for garden use. If the canes are allowed to grow to their full potential, however, the plants will be weakened, yield will be reduced, the fruit at the top will be difficult to pick and, if they are being grown in a fruit cage, the top netting may be damaged. The excess top growth can be pulled down and trained horizontally along the top wire for 25cm (10in) or so but any growth beyond that is best cut off.

PRUNING AUTUMN VARIETIES

The pruning of the autumn-fruiting primocane varieties is simpler still. They should be pruned during the second half of the winter by cutting all canes back to soil level. The new canes that bear the fruit will arise within a few weeks so there is never any necessity to distinguish between fruiting and non-fruiting canes.

FEEDING AND WATERING

The simplest feeding procedure is to apply 34g per square metre (1oz per square yard) of potassium sulphate shortly after mid-winter and then 70g per square metre (2oz per square yard) of either Growmore or fish, blood and bone two months later. On most soils, raspberries display symptoms of iron deficiency – yellowed leaves with conspicuous dark green veins. This can be remedied by routinely applying a proprietary brand of sequestered iron at the manufacturer's recommended dosage in spring. After the spring feeding, a thick mulch of well rotted manure or compost should be applied while the soil is moist. If the weather is dry, the plants should be watered as the fruit begin to swell; and the soil in the vicinity of the roots shouldn't be allowed to dry out.

WEEDING

The organic mulch will keep down annual weed growth close to the canes, at least in the early part of the season. If sufficient organic matter is available, it may be spread between the rows but some hoeing is usually still necessary too. The hoe should be used with great care, however, especially on thin soils where most of the raspberry roots will be close to the surface. Perennial weeds among established plants must be controlled with the translocated weedkiller glyphosate as any attempt to dig them out will inevitably damage the canes. Although a total weedkiller, glyphosate may be used quite safely among the crop if it is sprayed carefully on a still day and doesn't make contact with the raspberry foliage. If necessary, use a piece of cardboard as a temporary shield for the lower leaves on the canes.

The three most useful fertilizers for growing raspberries

YIELDS

Yields vary considerably between varieties (see p.46-49) and, to some degree, with the training system used, but as a rule of thumb, most modern summer-fruiting types should produce about 1.2-1.5kg per metre (2.4-3lb per yard) of row; primocane varieties less than half this.

HARVESTING AND STORING

Raspberries should be picked as soon as the fruit parts easily from the core. The maturing period will extend for a month or more within each variety (see chart, p.44) and so several pickings will be needed, even from a single variety. They can, of course, be eaten more or less immediately and will remain fresh in a refrigerator for about two or three days. They can be bottled, made into jams or preserves, or frozen.

A basket of freshly picked home-grown raspberries – what could be more rewarding?

RASPBERRIES

Symptoms of spur blight on raspberry canes; the only remedy is to destroy the infected canes

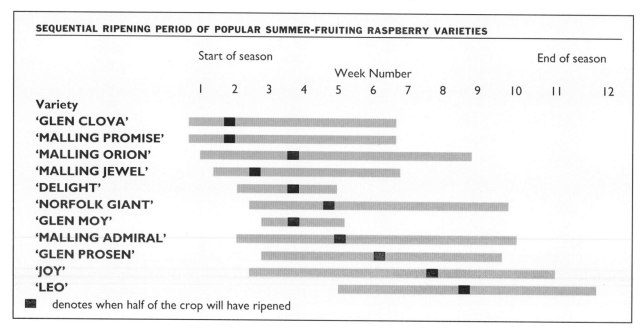

SEQUENTIAL RIPENING PERIOD OF POPULAR SUMMER-FRUITING RASPBERRY VARIETIES

Start of season — End of season

Week Number

1 2 3 4 5 6 7 8 9 10 11 12

Variety
'GLEN CLOVA'
'MALLING PROMISE'
'MALLING ORION'
'MALLING JEWEL'
'DELIGHT'
'NORFOLK GIANT'
'GLEN MOY'
'MALLING ADMIRAL'
'GLEN PROSEN'
'JOY'
'LEO'

■ denotes when half of the crop will have ripened

Varieties differ in their suitability for preserving (see p.46-49).

PROBLEMS

Unfortunately, raspberries probably suffer from more pests and diseases than any other type of soft fruit. Provided the plants are renewed fairly frequently, however, (see p.16) it is relatively unusual for cropping to be severely reduced. The following identification chart should be read in conjunction with my notes on p.30, where more general methods of avoiding and controlling problems are discussed.

Raspberry rust on the underside of a leaf surface

MAIN SYMPTOMS	CAUSE	TREATMENT
Fruit		
Small white larvae within	Raspberry beetles	Spray with contact insecticide immediately after flowering
Greyish powdery mould	Botrytis grey mould	Spray with sulphur or systemic fungicide
Crumbly	Virus or poor, dry soil	For virus: p.16; to improve dry soil: p.18
Leaves		
Powdery white covering	Powdery mildew	Spray with sulphur or systemic fungicide
Yellowish streaks and patterns	Virus	Renew plants if yield reduced
Tiny yellow, orange or black powdery spots	Rust	Collect and destroy affected leaves
Yellowed, veins dark green	Iron deficiency	See p.10
Wilting	Wilt	No treatment is possible; plant new stock on a fresh site
Purplish spots	Cane and leaf spot	Spray with systemic fungicide from bud burst onwards
Green or yellowish insects (aphids)	Raspberry aphids	Spray with contact insecticide
Pale fleck marks	Leafhoppers	No treatment recommended
Irregular holes	Caterpillars or sawflies	If severe, spray insects with contact insecticide
Many tiny holes	Capsid bugs	No treatment recommended
Canes		
Wilt, pink caterpillars inside	Raspberry moths	Apply tar oil spray in winter
Cracked and discoloured, pinkish larvae inside	Cane midges	Spray with contact insecticide in spring
Dark cracked patches close to soil level	Cane blight	As for cane midges, destroy affected canes
Dark purple patches (summer); silvery (winter)	Spur blight	Spray young canes with systemic fungicide; destroy old affected canes
Hard knobbly swellings	Crown gall	No treatment recommended

RASPBERRIES Varieties

Probably more than with any other type of soft fruit, the new raspberry varieties far outclass the older ones. While you may still see such old varieties as 'Lloyd George' offered by some nurseries, they have little to commend them today. And always buy plants, of whatever variety, that are certified as having been raised from virus-free stock.

Summer-fruiting varieties

'Delight'

'Glen Moy'

'DELIGHT' Early, pale orange-red, very large fruit, very heavy cropping, very vigorous. Poor pest and disease resistance. Not good for freezing or jam. Moderate flavour.

*'GLEN MOY' Early, no prickles, red, medium fruit, very heavy cropping, moderately vigorous. Some virus and aphid resistance. Good for jam and freezing. Good flavour.

'MALLING PROMISE' Early, red, large fruit, heavy cropping. Poor disease resistance. Good for jam and freezing. Moderate flavour.

*'GLEN CLOVA' Early to mid-season, red, medium-large fruit, heavy cropping for a long period, vigorous. Poor pest and disease resistance; best grown alone and should certainly not be planted with 'Malling Jewel' or 'Malling Promise', from which it will pick up virus infection (the virus is not apparent on these varieties). Good for jam and freezing. Moderate flavour, not very sweet.

'MALLING ORION' Early to mid-season, small red fruit, moderate cropping. Poor pest and disease resistance. Good for jam and freezing. Moderate flavour.

'GOLDEN EVEREST' Mid-season, yellow, moderate cropping. Good for freezing. Moderate flavour.

'MALLING JEWEL' Mid-season, dark red, medium-large fruit, moderate cropping over short period. Some frost, aphid, virus and botrytis resistance. Low vigour. Good for jam and freezing. Moderate flavour.

*'GLEN PROSEN' Mid-season, red, medium fruits, heavy cropping, moderately vigorous. Some virus and aphid resistance. Good for jam and freezing. Good flavour.

'MALLING ADMIRAL' Mid- to late season, dark red, large fruit, heavy cropping, vigorous, rather brittle canes. Some virus, cane blight and botrytis resistance. Very good for jam and freezing. Very good flavour.

'Glen Clova'

'Malling Jewel'

'Glen Prosen'

'Malling Orion'

'Malling Admirial'

'Malling Promise'

RASPBERRIES Varieties

Summer-fruiting varieties

'Augusta'

'GLEN COE' Mid-season, purple, medium fruit, heavy cropping, no prickles. Resistant to wilt disease. Good for jam. Moderate flavour.

*'LEO' Late season, orange-red, medium fruits, fairly heavy cropping. Some aphid and cane blight resistance. Very good for freezing. Very good flavour.

'NORFOLK GIANT' Late season, small red fruit, low cropping. Poor pest and disease resistance. Good for jam and freezing. Moderate flavour.

'STARLIGHT' Late season, black, medium fruit, low vigour. Good flavour.

'AUGUSTA' Late season, dark red medium fruit, heavy cropping, moderately vigorous. Some aphid and virus resistance. Good flavour.

'MALLING JOY' (often called 'Joy') Late season, dark red, large fruits, heavy cropping, very vigorous with widely arching laterals. Good aphid resistance. Good for jam and freezing. Good flavour.

'Leo'

'Glen Coe'

'Malling Joy'

'Norfolk Giant'

Primocane – Autumn-fruiting varieties

*'AUTUMN BLISS' Early autumn, red, medium fruits, heavy cropping. Aphid resistant. Moderate flavour. Easily the best of the primocane raspberries.

'ZEVA' Early- to late autumn, dark red medium fruits, low cropping. Moderate flavour.

'SCEPTRE' Mid-autumn, moderate cropping, moderately vigorous. Moderate flavour.

'SEPTEMBER' Mid-autumn, red, medium fruits, moderate cropping, moderately vigorous. Moderate flavour.

'FALLGOLD' Mid-autumn, yellow, medium fruit, low cropping. Good to freeze. Moderate flavour.

'HERITAGE' Late autumn, red, medium fruit, moderate cropping, vigorous. Moderate flavour.

* my top five garden raspberries

'September'

'Heritage'

'Zeva'

'Autumn Bliss'

BLACKBERRIES

" There are many gardeners who feel, with some justification, that a fine blackberry is the best-flavoured of any soft fruit; and I think I would probably agree. The biggest problem hitherto has been that the flavour of the garden varieties by and large fell short of that of the best wild blackberries. But simply planting a wild blackberry in your garden would soon result in an unmanageable tangle. Some of the newer cultivated varieties do approach the real wild blackberry in flavour, however, and although their flexible canes will always be a little more fiddly to train than the stiff ones of raspberries, the effort is well worthwhile. "

HISTORY AND TYPES OF BLACKBERRY

The wild blackberry or bramble is a very variable group of plants, a complex of numerous related species that botanists conveniently classify together under the name *Rubus fruticosus*. The group includes the typical flexible-caned brambles that you will find in the hedgerows and anyone who has picked wild blackberries from them will know how much one plant differs from the next in the size and number of fruit, the shape of the leaves, the vigour and in many other ways. One fairly distinct type is the dewberry, *Rubus caesius* and in North America this name tends to be used to distinguish the trailing types from some more erect, stiffer-caned forms called erect blackberries. The various garden varieties have been bred or selected from different species within

the overall blackberry group and among the more distinct types are the cut-leaved or parsley-leaved blackberries, derived from *Rubus laciniatus*, and a number of thornless types selected from *Rubus rusticanus inermis*. There are even types with very pale orange berries, called, would you believe, white blackberries. In recent years, some of the American upright-growing species have been used in European breeding programmes to develop new, more easily trained blackberry varieties such as 'Loch Ness'.

In common with raspberries, blackberries were not planted in gardens until relatively recently because wild fruit was always available and because the plant can be such an untameable monster. It was probably

not cultivated to any extent until the end of the eighteenth century but should certainly have a place in the modern fruit garden, provided care is taken in choosing an appropriately manageable variety. Most blackberries form their flowers and fruit on the previous season's canes, much like summer-fruiting raspberries although there are exceptions and the very vigorous 'Himalayan Giant', derived from *Rubus procerus* will form fruit on older canes too.

SOIL

Blackberries grow best in well drained, medium loam with a pH around 6.5 although they are moderately tolerant of slightly heavier soils. On very light and dry soils, they will be feeble and produce a small rather pathetic crop. Both heavy and light soils should be improved with organic matter before planting. However, it is scarcely worth persevering with blackberries on very thin chalky soils where the combination of water shortage and nutrient deficiency will always make a battle of their cultivation.

SITE

Blackberries are moderately shade-tolerant but will crop best and produce the sweetest fruits in full sun. They are particularly prone to damage from hard winter frosts and also from very cold winter winds and should therefore be given some shelter in cold or exposed areas. Planting them against a sunny, sheltered fence or wall is ideal, as only a few plants are likely to be needed and they are seldom required in such quantities as to necessitate planting long rows. New crops are always best planted

The ideal location for siting blackberries is against a sun-dappled fence

away from soil that has previously been used for growing other blackberries or related plants such as raspberries. In most areas, blackberries will require decent protection from birds. Ideally this should be provided by planting them in a fruit cage, although when they are grown along a fence or wall, other less sophisticated methods of netting them may be used.

PLANTING

Winter, especially early winter, is the best time for planting blackberries although they will establish fairly well at other times of the year. As they tend to be sold bare-rooted rather than in containers, however, summer planting is rarely an option. The planting hole should be dug at least 45cm (18in) deep and of similar width with plenty of well rotted

manure or compost and a handful of bone meal. Lightly trim the fibrous roots before planting, spread them evenly and plant with no more than 8cm (3in) of soil over them. If white shoot buds are present, these must be only just below the soil surface. Firm the soil carefully and slope it slightly away from the canes. Water well and top up with a mulch of manure or compost. Immediately

BLACKBERRIES

As can be seen from this wild blackberry, suitable supports and training are essential for ease of cultivation

after planting, cut back the canes to just above a bud about 25cm (10in) above soil level, if this hasn't been done by the nursery.

SPACING

In many gardens, a single plant will be sufficient to provide a modest crop but where several plants are grown, they should be widely spaced. The less vigorous varieties (see p.58) should be placed 2.5m (8ft) apart within the rows, with 2m (7ft) between rows. The more vigorous

types should be placed 3.5-4.5m (12-15ft) apart within the rows, with 2.5m (8ft) between rows. It is for this reason that I say many gardens will really accommodate only one plant. The major exception to this is the new, rather stiff-caned variety 'Loch Ness' which can be planted at a spacing of 1m (3ft) each way.

SUPPORTS

Almost more than any other type of soft fruit, blackberries must be carefully supported and trained.

Otherwise, not only will their canes make a tangled mass of growth, from which it will be very difficult to pick the fruit, but they will also be impossible to prune and the yields will, in consequence, be poor. All conventional training methods are best done with the plants supported against horizontal plastic-coated straining wire of approximately 10 gauge (see my general comments on p.12). Four wires should be spaced 30cm (12in) apart, with the lowest

Merton Thornless' a cultivated blackberry is a fairly vigorous variety and ideally should be spaced about 3-4m (10-13ft) apart within the rows with 2.5m (8ft) between the rows

BLACKBERRIES

Strong wire fed through stout wooden posts ensures support for the fruit laden branches of the blackberry plant

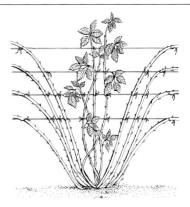

The fan system - single bay

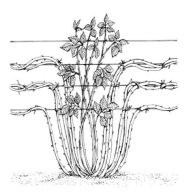

The rope system - single bay

1m (3ft) above soil level. The wires may be attached either to stout vertical posts or to vine eyes screwed to a wall or fence.

TRAINING METHODS

Numerous methods have been devised to train the long flexible canes but some are very difficult to do satisfactorily and I shall confine myself to two: the fan which, although rather time consuming to tie-in, is fairly easy to create and gives the highest fruit yield; and the rope which is very simple and quick to do but gives a considerably smaller crop. Both can be done on the single bay or alternate bay systems – two techniques designed to separate the new from the old canes. In the single bay method, the new canes that will bear next season's fruit are tied up through the centre and then out along either side and over the top of the old canes that bear the current year's crop. In the alternate bay method, the old and new canes are separated by training one batch to the left and the other to the right. If you use the single bay system, you should expect a slightly higher crop because the canes aren't quite so close together.

You will sometimes see rather more ornamental training methods used – over archways, for example, and there is no reason why you shouldn't experiment. But always bear in mind the need to keep fruiting and new canes apart. And of course, you will be unlikely with these decorative methods to obtain as big a yield or to keep birds at bay.

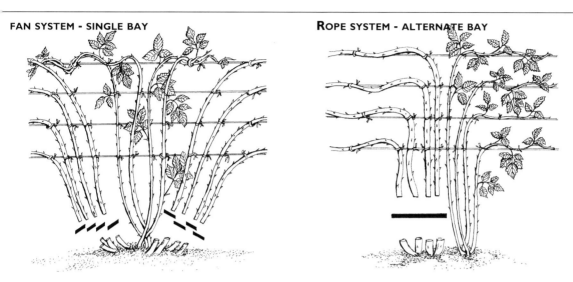

FAN SYSTEM - SINGLE BAY

ROPE SYSTEM - ALTERNATE BAY

With both the fan and rope systems, the old canes must be cut down in the winter and the new ones tied-in

PRUNING AND CANE THINNING

Pruning comprises cutting off the old canes at soil level as soon as they have fruited in early autumn. By this time, they generally look pretty unsightly. If you are using the single bay system of training, the new canes must then be retied in their place. With the alternate bay method, this isn't necessary. But with both systems, the young canes that emerge during the following spring will need to be tied, in turn, into their place. If the canes are much too long to fit into the horizontal space available, then cut off as much as is necessary from the tips.

On good soil, a very large crop of canes may be produced, especially from the more vigorous varieties but about 24 canes per plant is the maximum that should ever be retained. Any in excess of this should be cut out at soil level, selectively choosing, of course, the weaker ones for

removal. Suckers that emerge at a distance from the plant should be pulled away if possible; if not, then severed with a spade.

FEEDING, WATERING AND WEEDING

The same procedures may be used as described for raspberries (see p.42) although, in my experience, blackberries are much less prone to suffer any damage from hoeing too close to the base of the plants. However, if at all possible, any wild brambles growing in the vicinity should be cleared away, as they could operate as a potential source

Ripe and juicy blackberries, the reward for careful cultivation

BLACKBERRIES

When picking blackberries patience is needed as you will have to pick over them a few times. As here, some berries are ready, others need longer

of virus and other disease contamination for your plants.

YIELDS AND QUANTITIES OF PLANTS NEEDED

Yields vary greatly between varieties and also with the training method used. The best varieties, fan trained in good growing conditions may yield about 13-14kg (30lb) of fruit per plant, but in many gardens it will be much less than this. Yields will always be depressed by autumn frosts which bring fruit ripening to an end, so in areas where early frosts are to be expected, you should always concentrate on early-fruiting varieties.

HARVESTING AND STORING

Blackberries should be picked as soon as the fruit are truly dark. Several pickings will be needed over a period of a few weeks but it's wise not to pick in wet weather when the fruit are easily squashed and prone to grey mould rot. Because the fruit do not part from the plug and require pulling rather firmly, it is best to try to pick them by holding the stalk rather than the fruit itself. Blackberries will remain fresh in a refrigerator for about a week and can also be made into jam or frozen. However, freezing is a fiddly business because the stalk stubs must be cut off and the fruit do not, in any event, retain their form particularly well.

PROBLEMS

Blackberries are relatively free from problems. But any that do occur can be identified from the following chart alongside, which should be read in conjunction with my general notes on p.30-31.

Blackberry stem with purple blotch

A detail of stem rust on a blackberry plant

MAIN SYMPTOMS	CAUSE	TREATMENT
Fruit		
Small white larvae within	Raspberry beetles	Spray with contact insecticide immediately after flowering
Greyish powdery mould	Botrytis grey mould	Spray with sulphur or systemic fungicide
Crumbly	Poor, dry soil	Improve dry soil, see p.18
Leaves		
Tiny yellow, orange or black powdery spots	Rust	Collect and destroy affected leaves
Purplish spots	Cane spot or purple blotch	No treatment recommended
Pale fleck marks	Leafhoppers	No treatment recommended
Many tiny holes	Capsid bugs	No treatment recommended
Canes		
Pale purple spots	Cane spot or purple blotch	No treatment recommended
Hard knobbly swellings	Crown gall	No treatment recommended

BLACKBERRIES Varieties

There is probably more difference between blackberry varieties than between those of any other type of soft fruit because of the large number of species from which they have been derived. The only blackberry varieties for which certified virus-free stock is presently available are 'Ashton Cross' and 'Loch Ness' but others obtained from a reputable supplier should be perfectly reliable.

'Waldo'

'Bedford Giant'

'Black Satin'

*'**WALDO**' Very early, fairly heavy cropping, fairly low vigour. Very good flavour.

'**BEDFORD GIANT**' Early, very thorny, moderate cropping, very vigorous. Moderate flavour.

*'**BLACK SATIN**' Early, thornless (the earliest-cropping thornless variety), moderately vigorous. Moderate flavour.

'**FANTASIA**' Early to mid-season, moderate cropping but with very large fruit, vigorous. Moderate flavour.

'**HIMALAYAN GIANT**' Early to mid-season, very thorny, moderate cropping, extremely vigorous. Good flavour but better for cooking.

*'**LOCH NESS**' Early to mid-season, thornless, heavy cropping, low vigour with semi-erect habit. Plant only 1m (3ft) apart. Good flavour.

'**MERTON THORNLESS**' Early to mid-season, thornless, moderate cropping, fairly vigorous. Moderate flavour.

*'**ASHTON CROSS**' Mid-season, heavy cropping, fairly vigorous. Very good flavour.

'**JOHN INNES**' Mid- to late season, very thorny, moderate cropping, vigorous. Good flavour.

'**OREGON THORNLESS**' Mid- to late season, thornless, cut-leaved, low cropping, moderately vigorous. Moderate flavour.

'**THORNFREE**' Late, thornless, moderate cropping, moderately vigorous. Moderate flavour.

* **my top four garden blackberries**

'Fantasia'

'Himalayan Giant'

'Loch Ness'

'Merton Thornless'

'Oregon Thornless'

'Thornfree'

'Ashton Cross'

HYBRID BERRIES

" Having the best of all worlds is the philosophy behind the choice of hybrid plants, of whatever type. And cane fruits are no exception, for the best among them combine the attributes of raspberries with the attributes of blackberries, the two types most commonly involved in the crosses. But there are hybrids between other species too and the group also includes a few plants that aren't hybrids at all but unusual species in their own right. If you have room and are of an adventurous turn of mind, then you should grow at least one of these plants in your fruit garden. "

Kings Acre berry

Boysenberry

In the following list, maturing time is given in relation to black-berries and all should be cultivated in the same way as blackberries.

FRUIT Boysenberry
WHAT IS IT? Not known, but 'Himalayan Giant' blackberry was one parent.
APPEARANCE AND TASTE Large, purple, like an elongated rasp-berry, flavour good, blackberry-like.
SPECIAL FEATURES Early, vigorous, thorny, drought tolerant and a good plant for light, free-draining soils where other cane fruits fail. A thornless variety also exists.

FRUIT Hildaberry
WHAT IS IT? Cross between tayberry and boysenberry.
APPEARANCE AND TASTE Very large, red, flavour good.
SPECIAL FEATURES Very early, vigorous, thorny.

FRUIT Japanese wineberry
WHAT IS IT? A species, *Rubus phoenicolasius* from eastern Asia.
APPEARANCE AND TASTE Small, very pretty bright orange, flavour moderate and always said to be best when soaked in red wine, but in any event, makes an attractive addition to a mixed fruit dish.
SPECIAL FEATURES Early, fairly vigorous, very pretty with masses of soft prickles.

FRUIT King's Acre berry
WHAT IS IT? Cross between raspberry and blackberry.
APPEARANCE AND TASTE Medium, very dark red to black, flavour good.
SPECIAL FEATURES Early, fairly vigorous, thorny.

FRUIT Loganberry
WHAT IS IT? Cross between raspberry and blackberry, the oldest of these hybrids.
APPEARANCE AND TASTE Large, dark red, flavour very good.
SPECIAL FEATURES Early, fairly vigorous, the variety LY 59 is thorny but there is a thornless variant called LY 654.

FRUIT Marionberry
WHAT IS IT? Not known, may be a cross between raspberry and blackberry or a distinct species.
APPEARANCE AND TASTE Large, dark red to black, flavour good.
SPECIAL FEATURES Early to mid-season, very vigorous, very thorny.

FRUIT Phenomenal berry
WHAT IS IT? Cross between two American raspberries.
APPEARANCE AND TASTE Large, dark red, flavour moderate.
SPECIAL FEATURES Mid-season, fairly vigorous, thorny.

FRUIT Silvanberry
WHAT IS IT? Complicated cross, with boysenberry, youngberry, loganberry and marionberry in its parentage.
APPEARANCE AND TASTE Large, dark red, flavour good.
SPECIAL FEATURES Early to mid-season, very vigorous, thorny, claimed to be suitable for exposed, windy positions.

FRUIT Sunberry
WHAT IS IT? Cross between raspberry and a blackberry species.
APPEARANCE AND TASTE Medium, dark red, flavour good.
SPECIAL FEATURES Early to mid-season, very vigorous, thorny.

FRUIT Tayberry
WHAT IS IT? Cross between raspberry and a blackberry species.
APPEARANCE AND TASTE Large, dark red, flavour excellent, by wide acclaim the best of the raspberry-blackberry hybrids.
SPECIAL FEATURES Early, moderately vigorous, thorny, not very hardy and less successful in exposed gardens; always choose the certified virus-free 'Medana' strain.

FRUIT Tummelberry
WHAT IS IT? Cross between two tayberries.
APPEARANCE AND TASTE Large, dark red, flavour moderate.
SPECIAL FEATURES Early, but slightly later than tayberry, moderately vigorous, thorny, hardier than tayberry so better for more exposed gardens.

FRUIT Veitchberry
WHAT IS IT? Cross between raspberry and blackberry.
APPEARANCE AND TASTE Large, dark red, flavour moderate.
SPECIAL FEATURES Mid-season, moderately vigorous, thorny.

FRUIT Youngberry
WHAT IS IT? Cross between loganberry and dewberry.
APPEARANCE AND TASTE Large, dark red-purple, flavour moderate.
SPECIAL FEATURES Early to mid-season, moderately vigorous, thorny but there is a thornless variety too.

Japanese wineberry

From time to time, individual nurseries develop, import and/or promote other hybrid cane fruits. Among those I have seen in recent years but never grown are 'BLACKIE', 'RIWAKA', 'SMOOTHSTEM', the BLACK LOGANBERRY, the NECTARBERRY and the NESSBERRY. Rather few stay the course but if you are interested in experimenting, you should seek information on them from the suppliers. Among other frequently seen oddities are the JOSTABERRY and the WORCESTERBERRY which are not cane fruits but related to blackcurrants and gooseberries. They are described on pp. 72 and 83.

BLACKCURRANTS

"Blackcurrants have one big disadvantage and a few smaller ones for me; but in spite of this, they are among my most prized soft fruits. I must explain the contradiction. My main concern is that, in most seasons, most modern varieties are barely sweet enough to be eaten fresh without added sugar. Lesser problems are that most varieties make big, wide-spreading bushes and that, sooner or later, reversion disease will begin to decrease their yield. But against this can be set the facts that they make better jam and freeze better than any other soft fruit, they are relatively free from most other pest and disease problems and they are both easy to grow and prune. "

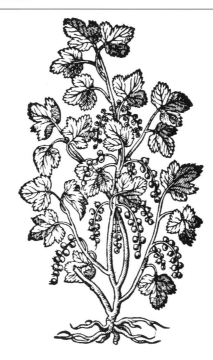

HISTORY AND TYPES OF BLACKCURRANT

Compared with red and white currants, the garden blackcurrant is botanically simpler in that, at least until very recently, it was derived from a single wild species. The wild blackcurrant, *Ribes nigrum*, occurs throughout much of central and eastern Europe and central Asia. In Britain, it's probably not a native plant but exists wild as an escape from cultivation. Like many other soft fruits, it was probably collected and eaten from the wild long before it was cultivated, and the blackcurrant wasn't described as a garden plant until medieval times when it was used for the flavouring and colouring of otherwise rather bland wine. It wasn't really until the eighteenth century that blackcurrants began to be used as a dessert fruit and even then many gardening writers shared my concern with its lack of sweetness. Subsequently, a large number of garden selections and crosses were made and, in recent years, other wild species have been used in breeding programmes to increase fruit size, pest, disease and frost-resistance and strig strength (the fruit stalk of currants is called a strig, although I have no idea why). Today, the blackcurrant remains much more popular in Europe than in North America, although its extremely high vitamin C content really ought to appeal to the health-conscious Americans.

SOIL

Blackcurrants tolerate heavier, slightly wetter soils better than most other types of soft fruit and will thrive in gardens where others fail. Heavy soils need less improvement to grow blackcurrants, although light, free-draining soils must have organic matter added. The ideal soil, however, is a deep, rich and moist loam, just on the acid side of neutral although it has always been my experience that they tolerate slightly alkaline conditions without detriment, and much better than most soft fruit.

SITE

The most important consideration is that blackcurrants are early coming into blossom and are very prone to damage from spring frosts. They must, therefore, have a sheltered position and should certainly never be planted in a frost pocket. I should add that one of the virtues of the newer varieties is that they are being bred to blossom later while managing still to crop early. Blackcurrants are moderately shade-tolerant but in any conditions other than full sun, it will be almost impossible to obtain fruit sweet enough to eat fresh. Although not as susceptible as raspberries or even red currants to bird damage, the most reliable crops will still be obtained from a fruit cage.

PLANTING

Blackcurrant bushes are available at different ages and sizes but much the best establishment will almost always be obtained from two-year old bushes. You can recognise these as they will usually have between four and six shoots. Smaller, one year-old plants will have at least two branches but will take longer to establish and begin cropping. Larger, three-year old plants will almost invariably have suffered too great a check to growth to be very successful. Be sure to

These commercially grown blackcurrants are planted in soil that is on the heavy side and has the added advantage of good protection and an open sunny position

BLACKCURRANTS

Young bushes which have established well are showing newly set fruit

obtain stock that is certified virus-free from a reputable supplier. It is very important to plant blackcurrants before mid-winter if at all possible (especially if they are being planted bare-rooted) because growth starts early and the tender young shoots will otherwise be damaged. Prepare a planting hole in the usual manner: about twice the size of the root ball and with well rotted manure or compost and a handful of bone meal well forked in. I have found the bushes respond better and produce stronger roots with animal manures than with compost. Blackcurrants should be planted deeply because new shoot development takes place

Given the correct amount of space in between plants, blackcurrants will flourish and produce an excellent crop

from the very base of the plant. Plant so that the soil just covers the basal fork where the lowest branches arise. This will be much deeper than anything you may be used to, but be assured that it is correct. Gently firm the soil around the plant, taking care to slope it slightly away from the bush. After planting, cut back all the shoots to a point just above two buds from the base.

SPACING

I've already mentioned the large size of blackcurrant bushes as a drawback and because of this they should be planted 1.5-1.8m (5-6ft) apart, depending on vigour, with the significant exception of the variety 'Ben Sarek' which is best at about 1.5m (5ft) but can be grown perfectly satisfactorily at a distance of 1.2m (4ft). I must say, however, that these spacings are not solely intended to obtain good growth, for the plants will crop quite reasonably at closer distances if they are well fed; but you will never be able to find room between them to pick the fruit.

SUPPORTS AND TRAINING

Uniquely among the commoner soft fruit, blackcurrants aren't amenable to being grown and trained in any way other than their natural bush form, for which they require no support at all.

PRUNING AND AFTERCARE

At the end of the first season, the number of branches on your plant should have at least doubled. Cut back one or two of the branches (depending on how many have been produced) to just above the base, as before, and also trim off to the base any additional weak and spindly

BLACKCURRANTS

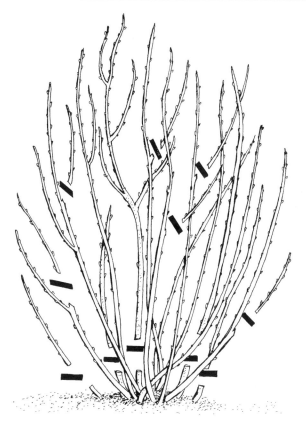

Every winter cut back about a third of all shoots to just above the base and cut off any spindly or damaged wood

shoots. The pruning thereafter is based on the fact that the best fruit will be produced on one-year-old wood with good crops also on two- and three-year-old wood but little of value on anything older. Each year, therefore, cut back between one-quarter and one-third of all shoots to just above the base, always ensuring that the oldest shoots and any emerging at a shallow angle are cut off first – they will hang down with the weight of fruit and simply drag on the soil. Also, cut off any spindly or damaged shoots. The pruning can be done any time between the fruit

reaching maturity and mid-winter but many gardeners find it useful to prune when the ripe fruit are still on the plant; the crop can then be picked from the detached branches.

FEEDING AND WATERING

Blackcurrants can be fed in the same way as most other soft fruit: apply 34g per square metre (1oz per square yard) of potassium sulphate shortly after mid-winter and then 70g per square metre (2oz per square yard) of Growmore or fish, blood and bone about two months later. The bushes should be well mulched directly after the second

feeding and then watered if the weather is dry at the time when the fruit are beginning to swell. It shouldn't be necessary to give sequestered iron unless the soil is very alkaline and old theories regarding the need to give extra large quantities of nitrogen to blackcurrants have been proved to be erroneous.

WEEDING

Although blackcurrants have a fairly extensive root system, damage can be caused to the young shoot buds by hoeing too close to the plant base. A wide band of mulch around the bush should keep down annual weeds in this area, and perennial weeds can, if necessary, be controlled with glyphosate (see p.42).

YIELDS

Modern blackcurrant varieties generally are high yielding and so few plants will be needed unless you want to have fresh fruit over a long period, when a succession of early, mid-season and late varieties is called for. Most varieties should yield at least 4.5kg (10lb) of fruit per season and unless they become affected with reversion disease, should continue to do so for 10 years or more.

HARVESTING AND STORING

Blackcurrants can be picked sequentially as they ripen, but this is a fiddly task and it is much better (especially if they are to be frozen or used for jam) to wait until all of the fruit on each bush is ripe. They will usually hang on the bushes for some time without dropping but to make the most of this, they really need to be in a fruit cage to prevent them being taken by birds. Although the individual fruit can be stripped as you pick

It is best to wait until all the blackcurrants are ripe before picking them

BLACKCURRANTS

These are the blackcurrants you can expect if you protect them well against birds and other pests

them, some will inevitably be squashed and it is much better to pick the whole strig and strip them later. Commercially, blackcurrants are harvested by machines that simply shake the bushes, and if bruising damage to the fruit is of no importance, then harvesting by manual shaking can be done in gardens, using either newspaper or old sheets beneath the bushes to catch the fruit. The compact and very heavy-cropping variety, 'Ben Sarek', responds particularly well to this method of harvesting. Blackcurrants will keep fresh for about seven days in a refrigerator but also bottle and freeze very well.

PROBLEMS

Reversion disease, the presence of which is betrayed by the symptoms of big bud, is easily the most serious of problems likely to affect your plants, although mildew can be troublesome on older varieties and in damp situations or where the plants are too close together. The following key to symptoms should be read in conjunction with my general notes on p.30-31.

A blackcurrant leaf suffering from aphid damage

Big bud caused by gall mite attack

MAIN SYMPTOMS	CAUSE	TREATMENT
Fruit		
Crop gradually diminishes year by year	Reversion disease	See Gall Mites
White or brown mould	American mildew	Spray with sulphur or systemic fungicide
Greyish powdery mould	Botrytis grey mould	Spray with sulphur or systemic fungicide
Leaves		
Powdery white or brown mould	American mildew	Spray with sulphur or systemic fungicide
Yellowish bands or patterns	Virus	Renew plants if yield reduced
Tiny orange or red powdery spots	Rust	Collect and destroy affected leaves
Green or yellowish insects (aphids)	Aphids	Spray with any contact insecticide
Many tiny holes	Capsid bugs	No treatment recommended
Tips twisted and distorted	Leaf midges	Destroy affected tips; no other treatment recommended
Buds abnormally large in spring (big bud)	Gall mites	Cut off and destroy buds; plan to bushes if yield begins to decline replace

BLACKCURRANTS Varieties

'Laxton's Giant'

'Black Reward'

'BOSKOOP GIANT' Very early, large sweet fruit, fairly low cropping, vigorous, spreading. Very good sweet flavour but frost susceptible. A very old variety that has retained its popularity because of its earliness and fruit quality.

*'LAXTON'S GIANT' Early, very large fairly sweet fruit, fairly heavy cropping, vigorous, spreading. An old variety with sweet fruit of large form that flowers early and is frost susceptible but has retained its popularity with show exhibitors.

'SILVERGEITER'S ZWARTE' Early, large fruit, fairly heavy cropping, vigorous.

'BLACK REWARD' Early to mid-season, large fruit, fairly heavy cropping, fairly vigorous, fairly spreading. Good fairly acidic flavour. Mildew susceptible, flowers about ten days later than 'Baldwin'. 'Tsema' and 'Tenah' are related Dutch varieties sometimes offered but 'Black Reward' is better for British conditions.

'BLACKDOWN' Early to mid-season, large sweet fruit, fairly heavy cropping, fairly vigorous, spreading. Good mildew resistance.

'SEABROOK'S BLACK' Early to mid-season, medium sized fruit, fairly heavy cropping, vigorous, spreading. Good resistance to gall mite.

'THE RAVEN' Early to mid-season, very large sweet fruit, fairly heavy cropping, very vigorous, spreading. A big plant but with the merits of very juicy fruit of good exhibition form.

'WELLINGTON XXX' Early to mid-season, large fairly sweet fruit, heavy cropping, vigorous, spreading.

*'BEN SAREK' Mid-season, very large fruit, extremely heavy cropping, moderate vigour, compact, upright habit. Very good flavour. Mildew resistant and, although flowering at the same time as 'Baldwin', much more frost tolerant. The finest garden blackcurrant and arguably the most important and outstanding soft fruit variety of our time.

'BLACKSMITH' Mid-season, large fruit, good fairly sweet flavour, heavy cropping, vigorous, spreading.

'GOLIATH' Mid-season, large sweet fruit, moderate cropping, vigorous, upright. A mid-nineteenth century variety that has been recovered and is now available as certified stock.

'Wellington XXX'

'Boskoop Giant'

'Blackdown'

'Ben Sarek'

'The Raven'

'Blacksmith'

BLACKCURRANTS Varieties

'Ben Nevis'

'Ben Lomond'

'BALDWIN' Mid- to late season, medium to large fruit, fairly heavy cropping, vigorous, fairly spreading. Good but acidic flavour, the standard variety by which all other blackcurrants are judged but always buy the selected 'Hilltop Strain'.

'BEN LOMOND' Mid- to late season, large, very juicy fruit, very heavy cropping, fairly vigorous, fairly upright. Good but acidic flavour, flowers about two weeks later than 'Baldwin' and usually escapes frost damage. Little mildew resistance.

*****'BEN MORE'** Mid- to late season, very large fruit, very heavy cropping, vigorous but upright. Good but acidic flavour, very late flowering and so escapes frost damage. Some mildew resistance.

'BEN NEVIS' Mid to late season, medium to large fruit, fairly heavy cropping, very vigorous, upright. Moderate, acidic flavour, fairly late flowering but slightly earlier than 'Ben Lomond'. Some resistance to mildew.

*****'JET'** (also calling 'Malling Jet') Late season, large fairly sweet fruit, moderately heavy cropping, very vigorous, spreading but with strong branches. Very good and fairly acidic flavour but one of the few modern blackcurrants that can reliably be eaten raw in most years. Flowers three weeks after 'Baldwin' so frost damage is not a problem. Some mildew resistance.

*****'WESTWICK CHOICE'** Late season, large sweet fruit, fairly heavy cropping, vigorous but neat and upright. A popular variety for exhibition.

'DANIEL'S SEPTEMBER' Very late, large, good acidic flavour, vigorous, spreading. Like several other old varieties, has remained popular because of its late cropping.

A number of new Scottish-bred blackcurrant varieties (all with the prefix 'Ben') and most with the later flowering characteristic that limits frost damage are being evaluated in commercial production and will gradually become available to gardeners.

JOSTABERRY A blackcurrant and gooseberry hybrid with huge, rather pale coloured fruit, very heavy cropping, vigorous and mildew resistant. Cultivate like a blackcurrant but for me, a curiosity to grow if you have room. Certainly not a substitute for a real blackcurrant.

* my top five garden blackcurrants

'Baldwin'

'Ben More'

'Jet'

'Westwick Choice'

Jostaberry

GOOSEBERRIES

" Quite why the gooseberry should share with rhubarb the dubious honour of being the butt of musical hall humour is beyond me. There is really nothing funny about this most individual of plants, although it has to be said that it is, overall, the least popular of all soft fruit. The reasons for this state of affairs aren't hard to find, for in most seasons many varieties never attain anything approaching the level of sweetness that would make them palatable as a fresh dessert. And, undeniably, a mouthful of sour gooseberry isn't an experience to repeat very often. The gooseberry is also a pretty unfriendly plant, its thorns making it one of the most difficult to pick, although it is very amenable to being trained in cordon fashion which renders both picking and pruning a much less hazardous exercise. "

HISTORY AND TYPES OF GOOSEBERRY

The name 'gooseberry' refers to a historic use of this fruit as the main ingredient for a sauce to accompany goose, the tart flavour compensating for the natural fattiness of goose flesh. The wild plant, *Ribes grossularia*, is common in many parts of Europe and North Africa but, like blackcurrants, those found in Britain are generally thought to be derived from old cultivated plants. And, indeed, the gooseberry has been cultivated for longer than most of its relatives in the *Ribes* genus. It's known that Edward I's fruiterer was purchasing bushes from France during the mid-

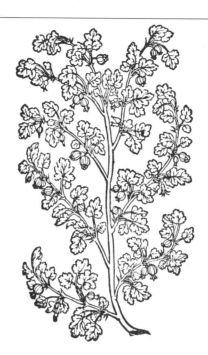

thirteenth century and selections from wild stock had been cultivated on the continent for some time previously. Curiously, they were at one time grown as ornamentals, primarily for the perfume of their flowers.

Although all were derived from the same species, several distinct types of gooseberry gradually arose: green-fruited, more or less pale green- or yellow-fruited, white- (very pale green) and red-fruited, all in varying shades, in varying sizes and shapes and with varying degrees of hairiness of the skin. The names of some of the old varieties betray these variations: 'The Hedgehog', 'The Blue', 'The Hairy Red', 'The English Yellow'. By the mid-nineteenth century, there were well over 300 varieties, and a new dimension and impetus was added to the plant's importance by the gooseberry clubs and competitions which sprang up, especially in

Lancashire and adjoining counties of northern England. Some still survive, and although there are now many fewer varieties of gooseberry in cultivation, there remain far more than any other soft fruit, although most are only available locally.

In recent times, gooseberry breeding has lagged behind that of other, more commercially important fruits but a number of different wild species have been used to develop varieties with mildew and aphid resistance as well as relative absence of spines. But for the traditionalist, a thornless gooseberry must surely remain an anathema.

SOIL

Gooseberries are versatile and will grow well on most soils provided they are not prone either to water-logging or drought, but will always be most successful on deep, moisture-retentive and slightly acid loams. Very light soils must be improved with organic matter. But one proviso must be made: gooseberries have a particularly high demand for potash and on soils such as light sands and

Winter planting for gooseberry bushes, gives them a head start

Here you can see just how many cordons of gooseberries can be squeezed into a relatively small area

also peaty and chalky soils with a low clay content, the symptoms of potassium deficiency will occur and so especial care must be taken to ensure that sufficient supplementary potash is given when feeding (p.18).

SITE

Gooseberries require shelter and will never crop to their full potential in an exposed windy site. This is partly because they come into flower very early and so are prone to frost damage, but also because the wood is brittle and will snap under the weight of fruit when blown by strong winds during the fruiting period. The buds and fruit are susceptible to bird damage and so gooseberries are best grown in a protective fruit cage. If the cage is small, the plants may be grown as cordons which take up very little room.

PLANTING

There are several forms in which gooseberry plants can be bought: bushes can be obtained as two- or three-year-old (or rather more rarely and less satisfactorily as one-year-old) plants, and either with single stems or as stools with several stems arising from close to soil level. The latter are cheaper, but unless you then go through the procedure of training one of the stems yourself to form a single stem or so-called leg, you will find they are much less easy to manage and pick from. Plants can also be bought with cordon or fan training already begun but these

GOOSEBERRIES

are relatively expensive and I much prefer to begin the training from scratch (an appropriate expression when referring to such a thorny plant as the gooseberry), and recommend that you do the same, as much as anything because you will then learn the basic principles involved.

As with other soft fruit, gooseberries establish best from winter planting. Early winter gives much the best results for the young shoots start into growth fairly early in the new season. Even when grown in a row as cordons, they are better when planted in individual holes of about 45 x 45 x 45cm (18 x 18 x 18in), rather than in a trench. Incorporate well rotted manure or compost with a handful of a general fertilizer, such as fish, blood and bone, that contains both potash and phosphate or alternatively, smaller amounts each of sulphate of potash and bone meal. Ensure that no air pockets are left between the roots by shaking the plant gently when refilling the hole

and firm it carefully, finally watering and topping up with a mulch of either compost or manure.

SPACING

Spacing between plants depends both on variety and on the growing system used. Free-standing bushes should be spaced 1.5-1.8m (5-6ft) apart, depending on vigour. Single cordons should be 30cm (12in) apart, double cordons 60cm (24in) and triple cordons 1m (3ft) with 1.2m (4ft) between rows if more than one row is grown. Fan-trained plants (see below) should be planted 1m (3ft) apart.

SUPPORTS FOR GOOSEBERRIES

Grown as free-standing bushes, gooseberries require no support. You will occasionally see them offered for sale as half-standards, the fruiting variety usually having been grafted on to a different rootstock and in such cases, of course, a stout permanent stake is necessary. For cordons, use a system of wooden

posts and horizontal wires, erected as for raspberries (p.39) although I find that three wires spaced 60cm (24in), 1m (3ft) and 1.2m (4ft) above soil level is the most useful arrangement. Fan training is unusual and not very easy to do although it can look most effective against a brick wall. It, too, is best done using horizontal wires as supports but I prefer to use more wires, the first being 30cm (12in) and the top one 1.5m (5ft) above soil, with three others, evenly spaced in between. Do bear in mind that protection from birds is very difficult to achieve with a wall-trained gooseberry.

TRAINING AND PRUNING

Bushes Think of the ideal bush towards which you are aiming as goblet-shaped with eight or 10 branches arranged around a more or less empty centre, ideally, as I have explained, atop a single stem about 25cm (10in) tall. If you have first to train this single stem yourself, it will generally add at least one year to the

TRAINING BUSHES

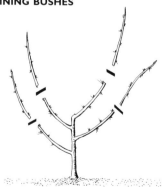

After planting, cut each branch to an upward facing bud, removing approximately a third of the branch

In the winter of the second year cut the leaders back again to form a good goblet shape. Remove any low-growing branches

In the winter of subsequent years, cut the leaders on each branch by a third and the side-branches to two buds from their base

overall operation. In the first winter after planting, cut out any branches in the centre of your goblet therefore and cut back the remainder by about one-third. Most varieties have a naturally spreading habit and these should be cut to just above an inward facing bud to encourage upright growth and a shape better able to support the fruit. Those with a naturally erect habit should conversely be pruned to above an outward facing bud to avoid branch congestion. I have indicated under each variety those which have a spreading habit and those which are naturally erect.

In the following summer, more branches will arise from those you have cut back and so in the next winter, repeat the cutting back until the required eight or 10 branches have been formed. Thereafter, in the second half of each summer, cut back each of the branches by about one-third and each of the side-branches that arise from them to about six leaf clusters from their base. In the following winter, further cut back the main branches by a third again and the side branches to two buds from their base. Cut out any wayward branches that arise in the centre of the plant and also the suckers that appear at soil level. This procedure is then followed year by year. From time to time, it may be appropriate to train a new branch to take over from one that becomes damaged or misshapen.

Some gardeners don't bother with summer pruning and do all of the cutting back in the winter. I find, however, that with a vigorous variety

TRAINING CORDONS

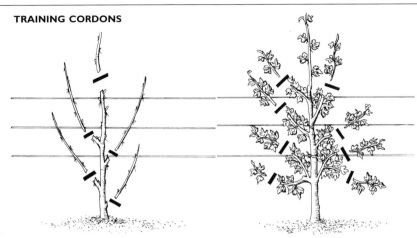

In the winter of the first year, shorten the main shoot by half, cut laterals to 2cm (1in) at a bud and cut out any low growth

In the first year after midsummer, cut the season's side-shoots to about the sixth leaf cluster. Leave the main shoot untouched

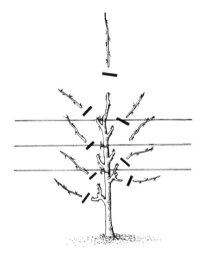

In subsequent years during the winter, cut the side shoots to 2 buds and the leader by a third

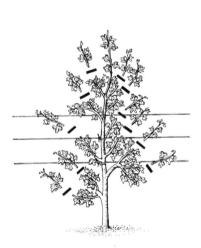

After midsummer cut the season's side-shoots to the sixth leaf cluster but leave the main shoot

on good soil, this can mean that there is a tangled mass of very thorny growth to deal with. It also means that for much of the season, the plant is congested and therefore more prone to aphid and mildew attack. But if you are to do summer pruning, make sure you leave it until

about six weeks after midsummer or you will simply encourage more and more side-branching.

Cordons Imagine a cordon as a bush with only one, two or three branches each trained vertically upwards and its pruning will make sense. If you don't buy a plant with

GOOSEBERRIES

A good organic mulch is important for the development of the fruit

TRAINING FANS

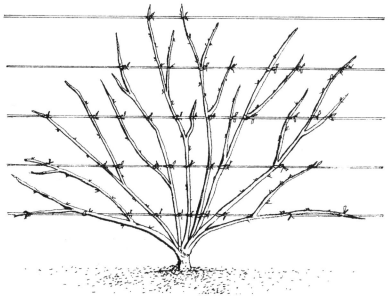

The major consideration with a fan-trained gooseberry is to ensure that the branches are spaced uniformly over the wall

the initial training done by the nursery, you must select the strongest and best placed vertical branches and cut out the remainder. Then, after midsummer, cut back all side-branches to just above the sixth leaf cluster but leave the main shoot untouched. In winter, cut the side shoots back to two buds from their base and the leader by about one-third until it reaches the top of its support wires when it should be treated in the same way as a side-branch. And that is all there is to it; the fruit will be much easier to pick, the plants will take up very little room, they will tend to be more disease-free because of the better air circulation around them and they will look very much more attractive than bushes too.

Fans Fan-training a gooseberry should only be undertaken if you are prepared to devote rather more than the average amount of time to the annual pruning and tying in. But having said that, there is nothing magical or intrinsically difficult about it; think of the fan as a series of cordons spread over a wall in a fan pattern and prune each of them in exactly the same way as you would a single cordon.

FEEDING AND WATERING

As I've already mentioned, gooseberries have an unusually high requirement for potash and this above all nutrients shouldn't be neglected in their routine feeding. I obtain good results by giving 34g per square metre (1oz per square yard) of potassium sulphate shortly after midwinter and then 68g per square metre (2oz per square yard) of

When weeding close to the bush do so with care as the root system is near the surface

GOOSEBERRIES

This shows just how many differences there are between gooseberry varieties; in colour, shape and size

Growmore or fish, blood and bone about two months later. After the second feeding, mulch with organic matter and then water if the weather is dry at the time the fruit begin to swell. Sequestered iron should only be necessary on very alkaline soils.

WEEDING

As with most soft fruit, weeding close to the bushes should be carried out carefully, for the root system is fibrous and extensive and much of it is close to the surface of the soil where hoeing or digging will cause damage. Hand weeding, mulching and careful hoeing should be used to control annual weeds and the weedkiller, glyphosate, used for any persistent perennials.

YIELDS AND QUANTITIES OF PLANTS NEEDED

Not many gardeners want the quantities of gooseberries that they do of most other types of soft fruit and the number of plants necessary in most gardens will therefore be relatively small. Most modern varieties should yield approximately 3.5-4.5kg (8-10lb) of fruit per bush and will continue to do so for much longer than other soft fruits; 20 years of productive cropping is not unusual. A single cordon should give 0.5-1kg (1-2lb) per season.

HARVESTING AND STORING

Gooseberries should be picked sequentially as they ripen when they will detach easily from the stalk. If they need to be pulled from the bush, then they are not yet ready. Gooseberries store well when fresh and will keep for around three weeks in a refrigerator and also freeze very satisfactorily.

PROBLEMS

The two biggest problems on gooseberries are American mildew and sawflies and while the former can, to a large degree, be avoided by careful choice of varieties, the latter requires extreme vigilance for they can strip the foliage in a trice.

Caterpillars, such as these of the magpie moth, can rapidly cause havoc

MAIN SYMPTOMS	CAUSE	TREATMENT
Fruit		
White or brown mould	American mildew	Spray with sulphur or systemic fungicide. If persistent, replace plants with resistant variety
Greyish powdery mould	Botrytis grey mould	Spray with sulphur or systemic fungicide
Leaves		
Powdery white or brown mould	American mildew	Spray with sulphur or systemic fungicide
Tiny orange or red powdery spots	Rust	Collect and destroy affected leaves
Green or yellowish insects (aphids)	Aphids	Spray with any contact insecticide
Many tiny holes	Capsid bugs	No treatment recommended
Small, dark angular spots	Leaf spot	Spray with systemic fungicide
Irregular holes, small brownish, caterpillar-like insects present	Sawflies	Pick off by hand or spray with contact insecticide immediately
Irregular holes, white, yellow and black caterpillars present	Magpie moths	Pick off by hand or spray with contact insecticide immediately

GOOSEBERRIES Varieties

'Early Sulphur'

'Invicta'

'Leveller'

'EARLY SULPHUR' Very early, medium-sized, yellowish, fairly sweet fruit, moderate cropping, vigorous, upright growth.

'MAY DUKE' Early, medium-sized, red, fairly sweet fruit, moderate cropping, fairly vigorous, upright growth.

*'INVICTA' Early to mid-season, large, pale green, fairly sweet fruit, very heavy cropping, vigorous, upright growth. Mildew-resistant.

'CARELESS' Early to mid-season, large, yellow, slightly sweet fruit, heavy cropping, moderately vigorous, spreading growth.

*'JUBILEE' Early to mid-season, large, yellow fruit, heavy cropping, vigorous, upright growth. An improved form of 'Careless'.

'WHITESMITH' Early to mid-season, large, very pale green ('white'), fairly sweet fruit, heavy cropping, moderately vigorous, upright/spreading growth.

'KEEPSAKE' Mid-season, large, green-white, slightly sweet fruit, heavy cropping, vigorous, spreading growth. Although mid-season ripening, its real merit is that the fruit swell very early and so it is the first to be ready for picking green for cooking. Prone to mildew.

'LEVELLER' Mid-season, large, yellow, sweet fruit, fairly heavy cropping, moderately vigorous, spreading growth. Prone to mildew.

*'WHINHAM'S INDUSTRY' Mid-season, large, dark red, fairly sweet fruit, fairly heavy cropping, vigorous, spreading growth. Very prone to mildew.

'GOLDEN DROP' Mid-season, medium-sized, yellow, slightly sweet fruit, moderate cropping, moderately vigorous, upright growth.

'LANCASHIRE LAD' Mid-to late season, large, red, fairly sweet fruit, fairly heavy cropping, fairly vigorous, upright/spreading growth. Some resistance to mildew.

*'HOWARD'S LANCER' Mid- to late season, large, green-yellow, slightly sweet fruit, heavy cropping, very vigorous, spreading growth.

'CAPTIVATOR' Late, small, dark red, fairly sweet fruit, fairly heavy cropping, moderately vigorous, spreading growth, almost thornless.

*'LORD DERBY' Late season, very large dark red, fairly sweet fruit, fairly heavy cropping, vigorous, spreading growth.

WORCESTERBERRY Late season, fairly small, very dark red, fairly sweet fruit, fairly heavy cropping, vigorous. A cross between a gooseberry and a blackcurrant.

BLACK VELVET A small, very dark red, fairly sweet fruit, fairly heavy cropping, vigorous. A cross between a Worcesterberry and 'Red Champagne' gooseberry.

* my top five garden gooseberries

'Careless'

'Jubilee'

'Keepsake'

'Lancashire Lad'

'Howard's Lancer'

'Lord Derby'

RED AND WHITE CURRANTS

" I have no hesitation in saying that these are the most under appreciated of all soft fruit, being far less widely grown than blackcurrants and even less than gooseberries. Both red and white currants have a distinctive flavour, similar to each other but different from blackcurrants. They are also remarkably heavy cropping and one plant of each, even a cordon, will provide sufficient for most people's needs. They are equally enjoyable, fresh or frozen and I hope that I can persuade all gardeners to give these very easy and rewarding plants the benefit of a trial. "

HISTORY AND TYPES OF RED AND WHITE CURRANT

Despite their markedly different colours, red and white currants are more closely related to each other than either are to blackcurrants, and are generally cultivated in exactly the same way as the gooseberry. Botanically, they are complicated because at least three wild species are involved in their ancestry, the individual species having given rise to distinct groups of cultivated varieties. *Ribes petraeum*, *Ribes rubrum* and *Ribes vulgare* are the three main species concerned, the latter two occurring wild in Britain, but unlike the other edible wild *Ribes*, they don't seem to have been either grown or collected as food until relatively recent times. By the sixteenth century, however, red and white currants were certainly popular in Holland, as they still are, and most varieties originated either from there

Prolific yields of fruit are produced by red and white currant cordons

or from France. Red currants, in particular, have become popular in North America, and are generally more widely grown there than are blackcurrants.

CULTIVATION

In all respects, the procedures that I've suggested for the cultivation of gooseberries applies to the growing of both red and white currants, see p.74-81.

YIELDS

So prolific are these plants that a double cordon of each, which is all that I have in my own fruit cage, gives more than enough for fresh and frozen use. Additional plants would of course be needed for juice production. A single bush should produce about 4-5kg (10-15lb) of fruit, a single cordon about 0.5-1kg (1-2lb) and, as they are not prone to reversion disease, they should crop well for at least 10 years.

HARVESTING

Always pick the fruit on the strig and separate them later if needed. You will simply squash them if you try to pull them off the plant individually.

PROBLEMS

The main disease problem is leaf spot (see p.81) and the main pests are gooseberry sawflies (p.81) and red currant aphids which give rise to reddish blister-like swellings on the leaves. The latter are most readily controlled by routine use of a tar-oil winter spray.

Leaf spot is the main disease to afflict red currants

There are few varieties available and not a great deal to choose between them except in respect of their maturing times:

RED CURRANT VARIETIES

'JONKHEER VAN TETS' Very early

'LAXTON NO. I' Early

'RED LAKE' Mid-season

'STANZA' Mid-to late season

'REDSTART' Late

WHITE CURRANT VARIETIES

'WHITE VERSAILLES' Early to mid-season

'WHITE GRAPE' Mid-season

'WHITE DUTCH' Mid-season

'Jonkheer Van Tets'

'Laxton No. I'

'Redstart'

'White Versailles'

'White Dutch'

STRAWBERRIES

"** I am very fond of strawberries, but I feel very concerned by the fact that a whole generation has grown up not really appreciating how a properly flavoured strawberry can taste. They have sampled mass-market, commercially grown and often imported fruits that bear little relation to the garden strawberries that I knew as I child, and indeed still cultivate. A good strawberry is not difficult to grow; it is largely a matter of choosing the right variety, but it has to be said that the best flavoured varieties tend to be the shortest-lived and it is a serious mistake to think of any strawberry in the same, long-term way as raspberries and currants. Think of them, in gardening terms, more as vegetables and you will be able to organize your strawberry growing to best effect. **"

HISTORY AND TYPES OF STRAWBERRY

As with other fruits, the taste of wild strawberries was first appreciated a very long time ago, but it was to be many centuries before they were first cultivated. The Greeks and Romans ate strawberries and there is evidence for them having been collected even earlier, in prehistoric times. The wild, so-called wood strawberry, *Fragaria vesca*, is a fairly common species of woodland edges throughout Europe and occurs also in the eastern part of North America. The name strawberry, doesn't incidentally, seem to have anything to do with the practice of

putting straw around the plants and long predates their cultivation. It probably comes from 'strayberry', for the runners cause young plants to stray from the parent.

Strawberries were probably first grown in gardens in the thirteenth or fourteenth centuries but for many years afterwards, especially in England, they differed little from the wild plants. There are other types of wild European strawberry: the small-fruited Alpine strawberry, a form of *Fragaria vesca*, is especially valuable as it has a much longer fruiting season; but the large-fruited summer garden strawberry we know today, owes its origin mainly to crosses made between two American species, the Virginian *Fragaria virginiana* and the Chilean *Fragaria chiloensis*. In turn, crosses between them and *Fragaria vesca* gave rise to the so-called 'ever-bearing' or 'remontant' strawberries which crop in summer and again in

the autumn. A huge range of large-fruited, summer-cropping varieties now exists but the appeal of the longer fruiting period of remontant strawberries has recently led to a number of new and improved varieties of this type.

A quite different type of strawberry, with a longer cropping season, is the Californian day-neutral. Here, unlike the traditional European strawberries, flowering and fruiting are not dependent on day-length, and a number of day-neutral varieties are now appearing in Europe. Planted outdoors in northern Europe, they behave pretty much like remontant strawberries but in warm climates or in greenhouses, they fruit virtually continuously. Their drawbacks are that they can really only be grown as annuals because the second year crop is very small and, by general consent, the flavour is not as good as that of the more familiar European varieties.

STRAWBERRIES FROM SEED

For many years, it's been possible to raise some of the small-fruited alpine strawberries such as 'Baron Solemacher' and 'Alexandria' from seed, but in recent seasons, a few day-neutral varieties have been introduced to European gardeners in seed form, too. The first was 'Sweetheart' but others, such as 'Temptation', have followed and no doubt many more will too. They are easy enough to grow. The seed is sown in the same way as for normal hardy annuals but the flavour will never be as good as that of the traditional large-fruited varieties.

Young strawberry plants in flower

SOIL

The best soil for strawberries is moisture-retentive, humus-rich and slightly on the acid side of neutral. In effect, this is the soil of a good vegetable garden and this further underlines the sense in thinking of strawberries more as a vegetable crop and less as a fruit. Heavy clay soils that have been improved with manure or compost are good for strawberries, but a very light, free-draining sand will need constant work and regular addition of organic matter if really worthwhile crops are to be obtained.

SITE

Strawberries must have sun, and the ideal site would be a very slightly sloping bed facing south. You will be unlikely to produce a satisfactory crop from a site that is shaded for longer than a small part of the day, and in such circumstances, I would strongly advise you to grow instead some perennial, small-fruited Alpine varieties such as 'Baron Solemacher' (p.97), which can even be grown as edging at the front of a herbaceous border. For the more traditional varieties that crop over two or three years, do take care to dig out any perennial weeds (couch grass especially) before planting as you will damage your plants by trying to do so later. Strawberries will tolerate a windy position but if the winds are very cold, you must expect some leaf browning.

ROTATION

Bearing in mind my suggestion to think of strawberries in much the same way as you would vegetables, you will realize that they need to be rotated; that is, each batch of plants should be grown on a different area of soil. This ensures that all of the nutrients in the soil are used to the full and, most importantly, that any soil diseases and pests have the opportunity to die away. Allowing at least four years before returning to the same plot is ideal. There are two ways to approach this.

STRAWBERRY ROTATING - *PLAN A* - Strawberries as a biennial crop using four plots and a four year rotation

	Plot 1	Plot 2	Plot 3	Plot 4
Year 1	Plant in Spring/Summer	(Other crops)	(Other crops)	Pick fruit in summer then remove plants
Year 2	Pick fruit in summer then remove plants	Plant in Spring/Summer	(Other crops)	(Other crops)
Year 3	(Other crops)	Pick fruit in summer then remove plants	Plant in Spring/Summer	(Other crops)
Year 4	(Other crops)	(Other crops)	Pick fruit in summer then remove plants	Plant in Spring/Summer
Year 5	Plant in Spring/Summer	(Other crops)	(Other crops)	Pick fruit in summer then remove plants
Year 6	Pick fruit in summer then remove plants	Plant in Spring/Summer	(Other crops)	(Other crops)
Year 7	(Other crops)	Pick fruit in summer then remove plants	Plant in Spring/Summer	(Other crops)

STRAWBERRIES

STRAWBERRY ROTATING - *PLAN B*
Strawberries as a longer term crop using two plots

	Plot 1	Plot 2
Year 1	Plant in Spring/Summer	Pick fruit in summer then remove plants
Year 2	Pick fruit in summer	(Other crops)
Year 3	Pick fruit in summer	(Other crops)
Year 4	Pick fruit in summer then remove plants	Plant in Spring/Summer
Year 5	(Other crops)	Pick fruit in summer
Year 6	(Other crops)	Pick fruit in summer
Year 7	Plant in Spring/Summer	Pick fruit in summer then remove plants
Year 8	Pick fruit in summer	(Other crops)

The simpler option is to grow your strawberries as an annual/biennial crop: plant them in the summer of one year to crop through the next and then dispose of them. If you choose this system, you should select varieties that really respond best to this approach and offer little in the second year: the old types such as 'Cambridge Sovereign' or, at the other extreme, the modern American day-neutral varieties. Next decide on the area that you are prepared to devote to strawberries (taking into account the yields you may expect – see p.91) and divide it into four equal plots. The planting and cropping schedule is then as I have shown in plan A.

If you decide that you don't want to go to the trouble and expense of replanting every year, you must choose varieties that will crop for more than one season and I suggest that you adopt plan B. This scheme is based on keeping the plants for three fruiting seasons before disposing of them.

Whichever system you decide on,

however, I would urge you not to try and grow a mixture of annual/biennial and longer-term plants because the planting and cropping scheme will then become hopelessly complicated.

Some protection from birds is highly desirable and the simplest way to achieve this is with lightweight fruit netting supported over the bed on short canes with upturned plant pots on top. A neater method is with a purpose-made strawberry net, supported on a light frame.

PLANTING

Strawberry plants are available from spring through to autumn but, in general, the earlier they are planted, the better they will establish ready for cropping in the following year. They are sold in various ways.

Freshly dug runners Either loosely packed in plastic bags or properly potted-up, usually sold in late autumn and early spring, depending on the severity of the weather.

Cold stored runners Dug in winter, with their leaves trimmed off and then stored in the cold to be taken

out for sale from spring to late summer. They won't establish well if planted later than this.

Potted-up cold stored runners These offer the most versatile option as they have been potted-up by the nursery and grown on in a greenhouse for planting from midsummer until autumn. They will cost more than bare-rooted runners but are much more dependable.

My experience has been that all pot-grown plants establish best if they are in bio-degradable pots which are then planted entire, allowing you to avoid the root disturbance that strawberries resent. The best nurseries will always pot-up routinely in this way.

About one week before planting, scatter Growmore or fish, blood and bone over the bed at 68g per square metre (2oz per square yard) and rake it into the surface. Plant pot-grown or bare-rooted runners with a trowel and firm them in very thoroughly, ensuring that the roots are all covered and that the crown is on the soil surface, not protruding. Water thoroughly after planting.

There is a good deal of nonsense talked about the need to remove the flowers from strawberries in the first year. I only find this necessary or worthwhile if they have been planted as bare-rooted cold stored runners. Pot-grown plants, put into a well-manured and fertilized soil will be perfectly strong enough to crop as they soon as they are ready.

SPACING

There is very often an inevitable disparity in gardens between the ideal spacing and what is practical. The

GROWING STRAWBERRIES WITH PLASTIC MULCH

Duty forces me to discuss this technique, although I hate covering the garden with plastic sheet. The principle is that used by many commercial growers: fairly heavy gauge black plastic sheet is laid over the soil before planting. It's essential to use black plastic as weeds will grow beneath a clear or translucent sheet. Either lay the sheet over the entire bed (and be prepared to walk carefully between the rows afterwards) or lay strips along each row, anchoring them at either side by burying the edges. Make slits in the plastic through which you can plant. The advantages are fairly obvious: weeds are controlled, soil moisture is retained, and the fruit are protected from contact with the soil. The disadvantage is that your strawberry bed will lose any pretence at being attractive and become purely functional. You will also have a great deal of dirty, waste plastic sheet to dispose of each time you move the bed; not an appealing notion in a green, recycling age.

A crop of ripe strawberries growing through black plastic sheeting

ideal is about 1m (3ft) between rows and 45cm (18in) between plants, but once the space demands of rotation have been taken into account, this can mean that a very large part of your kitchen garden is given over to strawberries, and 70-75cm (27-30in) between rows and 30-40cm (12-16in) between plants may be as much as you can manage. This will, of course, mean that you must take extra care when walking between the plants to pick the fruit.

GENERAL CARE

Apart from feeding and watering (p.91), strawberries need a modest amount of additional care. It's important to keep the fruit out of contact with the soil, otherwise they will fall prey to woodlice, mould and other problems. Although one way to avoid this is by growing the plants through a plastic mulch, a much more attractive method is the traditional one of laying straw beneath the plants as the fruit begin to swell. Tuck it beneath the plants so that it isn't blown around in the wind. Bracken is an acceptable alternative if it's available locally and it is now possible to buy proprietary strawberry mats, too. Don't, however, make the mistake of applying the soil cover too early for it will insulate the soil, trapping warmth within and making the plants vulnerable to frost damage on cold nights.

Immediately after the fruit have been picked, the old foliage should be cut off. This is most easily done with shears (I find single-handed shears the most convenient), and the plants should be trimmed to within a few centimetres of the crown where the new leaves will already be unfolding. The old straw from between the plants should be cleared away at the same time.

Perhaps the biggest confusion that gardeners have about strawberries comes in dealing with the runners – the stems that run along the soil surface, producing baby plants at intervals along their length. These will begin to form in early summer and if

STRAWBERRIES

Traditionally, the soil between strawberries is covered with a straw mulch to protect the fruit

An exemplary weed-free corner of a strawberry bed

A pretty display of container-grown plants, including strawberries

Although I have mentioned containers in general terms (p.28), strawberries are among the more obvious candidates for this type of cropping. You can either use one of the so-called strawberry tubs, usually made of terracotta or plastic and with holes in the sides, or alternatively an open wooden half-barrel or similar sized vessel. They are, I suppose, a fairly attractive option for someone who otherwise has no room to grow strawberries but they are far from ideal. You will need a great deal of good soil-based compost (John Innes No. 2 is ideal), the crop will inevitably be fairly small because most of the runners must be removed and the plants placed close together, so restricting them in size, watering will be a necessary and continuing chore and you may well have poor ripening. This is because half of the container will almost inevitably face away from the sun, unless it is small enough to be turned regularly. You will also have to help the pollination process by dusting over the open flowers with a soft paint brush; with relatively few plants, you must ensure that as many flowers as possible set fruit.

the plants are grown in a limited area at close spacings (p.89), the runners should be cut off as they grow. This allows each plant to concentrate its energies into developing the single crown. Where space is not limited, however, and the plants are wide apart, then you should retain about eight or ten runners from each plant and cut off the remainder. Allow them to root in the spaces between the plants, ideally arranging them so they are uniformly spread. You shouldn't, however, pot-up or transplant the runners to increase or renew your stock. They will not be reliably free from disease and, as always with soft fruit, it is much the best idea to begin with fresh certified virus-free plants.

FEEDING AND WATERING

Apart from the pre-planting fertilizer, strawberries should be fed in early spring with a light dressing of about 17g per square metre (½ oz per square yard) of potassium sulphate. If the plants have not cropped well, this should be repeated when the foliage is cut back after picking, but otherwise this second application is unnecessary. Watering is very important and in most years, additional water should be given regularly from the time that the fruit begin to swell until they have been picked. Watering earlier in the season than this will merely encourage leafy growth.

WEEDING

I have already pointed out the importance of clearing perennial weeds from the plot before planting and, thereafter, annual weeds should be controlled by hand. In a small, garden-sized strawberry bed, this is perfectly feasible and the hand fork should be the preferred method, as hoeing can easily damage the roots.

YIELDS AND QUANTITIES OF PLANTS NEEDED

From what I have said already, it will be apparent that is not easy to generalize about the yield of strawberries because it is tied closely to the

STRABERRIES

ORNAMENTAL STRAWBERRIES

Although there have been more or less ornamental varieties of *Fragaria* in cultivation for some years, most notably those with variegated foliage, more recent arrivals in nursery catalogues have been related species or varieties grown for their pink flowers rather than their fruit. 'Pink Panda' is the best known and has proved very popular as a front-of-border perennial. It will form the occasional fruit, too, but should not be grown as a fruiting substitute for real strawberries. Some of the newer ornamental strawberries due to appear over the next few years promise something more of a real crop. Rather different and much older is 'Variegata' which has the appeal of white-blotched leaves. The flowers are white and the fruit small but palatable.

One of the newer ornamental strawberries now available, 'Serenate'

varieties grown, the type of planting stock, the time that they are planted, the spacing adopted and the number of years over which they are cropped. My experience, however, is that a high-yielding commercial variety, such as 'Cambridge Favourite',

the most popular in Britain, planted early as pot-plants should produce about 450g (1lb) of fruit per plant in its first cropping year if grown as single-spaced plants with the runners removed. Most families' needs, should be satisfied by 25-35 plants.

EXTENDING THE STRAWBERRY SEASON

Uniquely among commonly grown soft fruit, the season for strawberries can be extended, even without a greenhouse, because the plants are small enough to be covered with

cloches. Glass cloches put over the plants about two months after midwinter will advance the first ripening by up to a month. Plastic cloches will give about two weeks advance. When using cloches of any type, however, it's important to provide some ventilation or botrytis grey mould will become a problem.

If you enjoy fresh strawberries and have a greenhouse, you can produce fruit for about eight months of the year. Use the following chart to plan your long-term strawberry crop.

Time for fruit to ripen	How to grow them	Where to grow them
MID- TO LATE SPRING	Plant pot-raised plants into large containers in late summer	Cold greenhouse
LATE SPRING	Plant pot-raised plants in late summer	Outdoor beds, covering with cloches in late winter
EARLY SUMMER	Plant pot-raised plants between midsummer and autumn	Outdoor beds
EARLY AUTUMN	Plant pot-raised, autumn-fruiting varieties in autumn or spring	Outdoor beds
LATE AUTUMN TO WINTER	Plant pot-raised day-neutral varieties in containers in spring	Greenhouse @ 10°C (50°F)

HARVESTING AND STORING

Strawberries for immediate use or to be used for freezing or jam making should be picked when the fruit are uniformly red; they will only keep fresh for a couple of days in this condition. Unless they are to be used within a few hours, they should be picked complete with the calyx. The storage time can be extended by picking partly ripe fruit which will keep for up to a week or more in a refrigerator, but will never be as sweet and tasty. It is because commercial crops are usually picked this way that strawberries bought at a supermarket are rarely as sweet as those which are freshly picked from your own garden.

Although varieties do differ slightly, no strawberry will ever emerge from a freezer with exactly the same shape, texture or flavour as when they were fresh, and for this reason, if you choose to freeze the fruit, then they are best re-used for cooking purposes.

PROBLEMS

Like any vegetatively propagated crop, strawberries are prone to virus diseases but these are generally not very serious because the plants are grown for such a relatively short time. The succulent fruit are as attractive to pests and moulds, however, as they are to us. Use the following chart in conjunction with the general notes on p.30.

Strawberry fruit fall prey to several different moulds in damp weather

MAIN SYMPTOMS	CAUSE	TREATMENT
Fruit		
Large holes or pieces removed	Slugs, snails or birds	Use slug traps and cover plants with nets
Tiny holes, seeds eaten	Strawberry beetles	Clear away all debris in autumn. Sink jars in soil between plants to trap insects
Greyish powdery mould	Botrytis grey mould	Spray with sulphur or systemic fungicide, as preventative immediately after flowering in the following season
Leaves		
Powdery white mould	Mildew	Destroy severely affected plants and put new stock on a different site
Green or yellowish insects (aphids)	Aphids	Spray with any contact insecticide
Various dark spots	Leaf spot diseases	Take care to clear away all dead foliage after cropping
Pale coloured, veins dark green	Iron deficiency	Apply sequestered iron in early spring
Brown or bronzed with cobwebs present	Red spider mites	Chemical control is impractical. Keep plants well mulched but destroy them if severe symptoms persist
Distorted	Strawberry mites	Destroy severely affected plants and put new stock on a different site
Plants		
Distorted	Strawberry mites	See above
Wilt and then die, white larvae in soil	Weevils	See strawberry mites

STRAWBERRIES Varieties

There are far more varieties of strawberry than any other soft fruit and the following selection covers the best and most popular. Individual nurseries import and supply many others but few last on the lists for more than a few seasons.

Large fruited, summer cropping varieties

'Pantagruella'

'Tamella'

'Hedley'

'PANTAGRUELLA' Very early, neat, compact plants, good under cloches but prone to mildew later in season. Moderate cropping, flavour moderate but useful because so early.

'TAMELLA' Early in first year, early to mid-season in second year. Heavy cropping, and can reliably be cropped for three years on good soils.

'HEDLEY' Early to mid-season, compact, upright, not very sweet but very good for preserving.

'HARVESTER' Early to mid-season, heavy cropping, upright, vigorous, flavour moderate.

'RED GAUNTLET' Early to mid-season, heavy cropping, flavour moderate, will produce a second crop in good summers.

'TANTALLON' Early to mid-season, heavy cropping, flavour moderate. Suffers in dry seasons, good disease resistance.

'SILVER JUBILEE' Early to mid-season, flavour good, open habit, moderate cropping.

*'ROYAL SOVEREIGN' Early to mid-season, the old variety with the flavour by which others are judged, low cropping. Disease-prone, crop for one year only.

'BOUNTY' Mid-season, heavy cropping, good flavour, crop for two years only.

*'CAMBRIDGE FAVOURITE' Mid-season, the standard British commercial variety, heavy cropping, long cropping period. Resistant to mildew, prone to red spider mite which can very troublesome in dry areas and hot summers.

'ELSANTA' Mid-season, heavy cropping, moderate flavour, prone to disease.

'Harvester'

'Red Gauntlet'

'Silver Jubilee'

'Elsanta'

'Royal Sovereign'

'Tantallon'

'Cambridge Favourite'

'Bounty'

STRAWBERRIES Varieties

Large fruited, summer cropping varieties

'Tenira'

'TENIRA' Mid-season, moderate cropping, good flavour, upright habit, crop for one year only.

'TOTEM' Mid-season, moderate cropping but the best for freezing as it retains its shape afterwards better than other varieties.

'SALADIN' Mid- to late season, very heavy cropping, moderate flavour. Resistant to mildew.

'TROUBADOUR' Mid- to late season, poor in dry summers, flavour moderate, fairly heavy cropping. Good disease resistance.

'PEGASUS' Late season, heavy cropping, good flavour. Good disease resistance.

'PANDORA' Late season, heavy cropping, moderate flavour. Good disease resistance. Uniquely, not self-fertile so must be grown with another variety such as 'Cambridge Favourite'.

'Totem'

'Saladin'

'Troubadour'

'Pandora'

Remontant varieties

*'**AROMEL'** Moderate cropping, very good flavour, crops twice but to obtain the best benefit from the autumn crop, remove the first flowers in late spring. This is the remontant variety that the others have to beat.

'**OSTARA'** Moderate cropping, moderate yield. Fairly low disease resistance.

'**RABUNDA'** Moderate cropping, fairly good flavour. Low disease resistance.

'**RAPELLA'** Fairly heavy cropping, good flavour. Low disease resistance and best in warmer areas.

'Aromel'

Day-neutral varieties

Among the varieties introduced so far to Europe are '**SELVA'**, '**FERN'**, '**TRIBUTE'** and '**TRISTAR'**. They are similar, one-year only plants, fairly heavy cropping but with very moderate flavour.

Alpine varieties

*'**BARON SOLEMACHER'** Good, sweet flavour, fairly heavy cropping for an Alpine but with very tiny fruits.

'**ALEXANDRIA'** Sweet flavour, larger but fewer fruits than 'Baron Solemacher'

'**YELLOW WONDER'** Fairly good flavour, moderate cropping but with the real appeal of little yellow fruits

* **my top four garden strawberries**

'Alexandria'

'Baron Solemacher'

ACID SOIL FRUITS

❝It remains something of a mystery to me why the acid soil fruits should be so much more popular in North America than in Britain and continental Europe. Surely it can't be that there are proportionately more gardens with acid soils in the US. Whatever the answer, there is certainly no reason why any garden with peaty, naturally acid soil (especially in milder, wetter areas) shouldn't grow at least the two most popular types, blueberries and cranberries. But I do have to say that if your garden soil isn't already on the acid side of neutral, please don't be tempted to add tons of peat or sulphur or to try and render it so. ❞

HISTORY AND TYPES OF ACID SOIL FRUIT

Although they are very different in appearance, both blueberries and cranberries belong to the same genus, *Vaccinium*, in that classic acid soil plant family, the Ericaceae. It is also however a group of plants in which the common names have become very confusing, with the same name used for more than one species.

The blueberry that interests us here is *Vaccinium corymbosum*. Because of its size, it is sometimes called the highbush blueberry to distinguish it from lower-growing types. It is native to the eastern United States, where a related species *Vaccinium australe* has been hybridized with it. The highbush blueberry reaches about 3.5m (11ft)

in height and although the fruits were collected from the wild in North America by both native Americans and European settlers, their cultivation didn't really begin seriously until the early years of the present century. Much breeding has been performed since and some of the newer varieties have far greater cold tolerance.

The cranberry is at the other end of the size spectrum being a wiry, creeping plant. There are wild European cranberries, most notably *Vaccinium oxycoccos* and *Vaccinium vitis-idaea*, but they are small-fruited and not commonly grown in gardens. The cultivated varieties have all arisen during the present century and are derived from the larger and more juicy-fruited American cranberry *Vaccinium macrocarpon*. Cranberries are an important commercial crop in the United States but are more difficult than blueberries to grow well in gardens.

In passing, I should add that the fruits of a related group of plants, in the genus *Gaylussacia*, are popularly collected from the wild in North America and sometimes grown in American gardens. These are the huckleberries, immortalized in the name of Mark Twain's hero, but unfortunately they are rarely available from European nurseries.

Bright red, ripe cranberries

Commercially grown blueberries in mid-winter showing their attractive bark

Blueberries

*❝ The very name almost prompts you to burst into patriotic Rodgers and Hammerstein, for the blueberry is a plant that has truly wound its way into American folk culture. It finds its greatest glory in blueberry pie but it also makes a very worthwhile garden plant if you have room and patience. Patience is certainly needed, because it will be at least two years before the plants begin to crop and five or more before they are in full bearing. The fruits do genuinely appear pale blue, because the waxy bloom lightens the dark blue-black skin colour. For those more used to seeing their wild European relative, the bilberry (*Vaccinium myrtillus*), blueberries are large, 2cm (1in) or more in diameter and, although less than exciting when raw, they do cook wonderfully well. While you wait for the bushes to come into full bearing, however, the beautiful yellows and reds of the autumn leaf colours will provide ample enjoyment and I have always felt that this is a plant worthy of a place in the ornamental shrub border in its own right. ❞*

SOIL

It is, of course, the soil that is the key to growing blueberries. It must be moist but well drained (and preferably, therefore, in a high rainfall area) and above all, acidic, with a pH of 4-5.5. The ideal is an acidic sandy loam; a garden where the soil is rather too acid to grow good vegetables will generally be a good blueberry prospect. Given a natural pH of up to about 6.5 and otherwise good conditions, it is worth adding sulphur to increase the acidity (see chart over page). Otherwise, they may be grown in large containers about 45 x 45 x 45cm (18 x 18 x 18in) of ericaceous compost.

SITE

Blueberries require a sunny position, with adequate shelter from strong and cold winds and also freedom from late frosts that will damage the blossom must be taken into account. The bushes themselves can be damaged by cold, penetrating winter frosts. As birds do not usually present a problem, blueberries need not be grown in a fruit cage or with any other special type of protection.

PLANTING AND SPACING

Blueberries should always be bought as container-grown plants for they do not transplant satisfactorily if bare-rooted. Two-year-old plants will establish best and should be planted in winter, in soil well supplied with organic matter, at a spacing of 1.2-1.5m (4-5ft) between plants and 1.5-1.8m (5-6ft) between rows. Don't plant the bushes any deeper than the soil mark on the stem. Water thoroughly.

FEEDING AND WATERING

Blueberries must be mulched and this is best done with coniferous sawdust which breaks down slowly and increases the soil acidity as it does so. Somewhat ridiculous depths of mulch are sometimes suggested but 15cm (6in) is reasonable. They

If ideal conditions are provided, blueberries will give you a good yield

require little feeding: 17g per square metre (½oz per square yard) each of potassium sulphate and ammonium sulphate in the early spring. Maintain the soil in a moist state during dry periods.

WEEDING

More than almost any other soft fruit, blueberries resent root disturbance, so weeding between the bushes must be performed very carefully. The sawdust mulch should maintain the area close to the plants weed-free.

PRUNING

Blueberries are grown as stooled bushes and their pruning is identical to that applied to blackcurrants (p. 65), the main principle being to stimulate the regular production of new shoots and growth from the base of the plant

YIELDS AND QUANTITIES OF PLANTS NEEDED

As I've mentioned, blueberries are slow to come into full bearing but after about six years, a bush should yield 2.5-3.5kg (6-8lb) of fruit. They should continue to crop for 20 years or more.

ACID SOIL FRUITS

HARVESTING AND STORING

The cropping season is a long one, from late summer until early autumn but the fruit don't ripen uniformly and the bushes must be picked over every few days. Place a hand under each cluster of berries and roll them in the palm. The ripe fruits detach easily. Blueberries will keep fresh for about three weeks in a refrigerator and freeze very well.

PROBLEMS

Blueberries are almost trouble-free. Leaf yellowing can occur if the soil pH rises but can be checked by applying a fertilizer containing sequestered iron in the spring. The only significant disease problem is a canker that appears as dark stem lesions with red and yellow margins. Affected parts should be cut out and destroyed. Botrytis grey mould may affect the fruits as they swell but can be checked by spraying with sulphur or a proprietary systemic fungicide.

Blueberries are all self-fertile but, mainly because the flowers don't open uniformly, it's wise to have two varieties to achieve the best pollination.

Blueberry varieties

'BLUETTA' Very early, moderate flavour, heavy cropping, moderately vigorous.

'EARLIBLUE' Early, good flavour, large, pale blue fruits, moderate cropping, vigorous, upright.

*'BLUE CROP' Early to mid-season, good flavour, fairly heavy cropping, vigorous, upright.

'BERKELEY' Mid-season, good flavour, heavy cropping, vigorous, spreading.

'IVANHOE' Mid-season, good flavour but small dark fruits, vigorous, upright. Resistant to canker.

'COLVILLE' Late, good flavour, heavy cropping, vigorous, spreading.

* **my top all-round blueberry**

'Berkeley'

'Bluetta'

'Blue Crop'

'Ivanhoe'

QUANTITIES OF SULPHUR TO ADD TO SOILS TO INCREASE THE ACIDITY TO pH 4		
Natural pH	Light, free-draining soil	Medium, more retentive soil
5.5	34g per square metre	78g per square metre
6.5	78g per square metre	156g per square metre
n.b. 34g per square metre = 1oz per square yard		

Cranberries

❝ *I suppose the fact that cranberry sauce is so frequently served with turkey explains why the plant has become so important in North America.*

It is a pretty little thing, especially when in fruit, its wiry stems winding their way over the soil surface and studded at regular intervals with bright red jewel-like berries, each slightly over 1cm (½in) in diameter.

It isn't easy to grow in gardens, the key to success being to remember that its natural habitat is close to acidic bogs; and bogs mean water. ❞

'C.N.'

'Franklin'

SOIL AND SITE

The soil should be as for blueberries but, if anything, even more acidic (as low as a pH of 3.5), organic and wetter but still free-draining. This necessitates either a high rainfall or a supply of soft water to supplement it. It's worth bearing in mind that even if your garden soil is very acidic, you may still have hard (limey) tap water that is piped from an area of alkaline rocks so stored rainwater should be used. An ideal position for a cranberry bed would be in a bog garden on a peaty soil.

PLANTING AND AFTERCARE

As with blueberries, always buy container-grown young plants and never allow them to dry out. Plant in winter no deeper than the soil mark on the stem. Spreading a layer about 2cm (1in) deep of lime-free sand over the bed after planting will help the plants to establish and prevent the surface organic matter from drying out. The sand should also be used to hold down the trailing stems until they root. Space the plants 30cm (12in) each way and you should obtain a yield from an established bed of about 0.5kg per square metre (1lb per square yard) .

Cranberries will grow well with no artificial feeding although 17g per square metre (½oz per square yard) of sulphate of ammonia should be given in early spring if growth in the previous season has been poor. No pruning is needed but any aerial shoots should be trimmed in spring.

HARVESTING AND STORING

Cranberries are extremely fiddly to pick so it is wise to wait until more or less all of the fruit have ripened, and then pick them in one session. Despite their fragile appearance, they keep very well – for two months or more in a refrigerator – and keep their shape if frozen.

PROBLEMS

Slight aphid infestation is the only pest and disease problem likely to be encountered on cranberries growing in Europe.

Cranberry varieties

From limited trials in Scotland, the best cranberries for garden conditions have proved to be the American varieties, **'C.N.'** with large red fruit and a free mat-forming habit, and **'FRANKLIN'** with smaller, darker fruits and a less vigorous spread. Most specialist suppliers should have at least one of these, although you will have to make do with others if these are unavailable. **'EARLY BLACK'** and the late season variety **'McFARLIN'** are probably the best of the rest.

CAPE GOOSEBERRIES

"Physalis peruviana once gave me one of my most pleasurable broadcasting experiences. I was sitting on the terrace of a lovely garden in southern England, interviewing its owner, an erstwhile television reporter from Hawaii, who proceeded to serve tea and scones, accompanied by a splendid preserve. It was a delicious jam that she had made from the fruits of the plant that Europeans tend to call the Cape Gooseberry. Subsequently, I have grown it many times and have come across it more and more frequently in restaurants and supermarkets. It makes a useful addition to the very limited number of half-hardy fruit crops, since it is easy to grow, either annually from seed or as a greenhouse perennial to be cut down each autumn. In appearance, the fruits resemble small orange cherries, encased in a papery calyx that betrays the plant's relationship to the ornamental Chinese lantern."

Plant Cape gooseberries outdoors after the risk of frost has passed

HISTORY AND TYPES OF PHYSALIS

There are several closely related edible species of *Physalis*, all from warm parts of the New World. They are often confused with each other and have common names that seem to be almost interchangeable. The true Cape gooseberry is a tender perennial, while the commonest of the others is an annual, *Physalis pubescens*, most usually called the strawberry tomato. But to confuse matters, *Physalis pubescens* is also sometimes called the ground cherry, as are at least four other species, including, on occasion, *Physalis peruviana*. At least two others are known as jam berries, at least two more are called tomatillos and two more are known as husk tomatoes. To add final confusion, there are both orange- and purple-fruited forms within some of the species. They were, no doubt, all eaten by native American peoples and *Physalis peruviana* has been grown in Europe since the late-eighteenth century.

WAYS TO GROW CAPE GOOSEBERRIES

If you can grow bush tomatoes, then you can grow Cape gooseberries. In a greenhouse, they can be cultivated in growing bags or by ring culture, but are probably most easily grown in 20cm (8in) diameter pots of soil-based John Innes No. 2 potting compost. Outdoors, they should be grown in well prepared beds into which compost or well rotted manure has been dug in advance. Rake in a general balanced fertilizer about one week before planting. It makes sense to place tall cloches over the plants in the early stages.

Sow two seeds to each 9cm (3½in) pot of soil-based sowing compost in warmth and pull out the weaker if both germinate. Sow about six weeks before you wish to plant; outdoors, you can plant immediately after the risk of the last frost has passed. In a greenhouse maintained at a minimum temperature of about 7°C (45°F), you should be able to plant some four to six weeks earlier. After transplanting, insert a stout cane close to each plant and tie them in as they grow. Pinch out the growing tip when the plants reach about 45cm (18in) in height to encourage bushiness. There is no need to remove side-shoots.

FEEDING AND WATERING

Don't allow the compost to dry out, and give a proprietary liquid tomato fertilizer to greenhouse plants once a week after the first fruit have set, following the manufacturer's recommendations as given for tomatoes. Outdoor plants should be fed once every two weeks at the most.

HARVESTING AND STORING

Cape gooseberries are ripe when the calyx becomes very papery and the fruit inside is richly coloured. They will keep for several weeks after picking and may then be eaten fresh, simply by peeling back the calyx, or, as I have already suggested, made into delicious jam.

PROBLEMS

Whiteflies and aphids may be troublesome, especially in greenhouses.

Cape Gooseberry varieties

Although a number of named varieties exist in North America, I haven't seen these offered in Europe where some nondescript name such as **'GOLDEN BERRY'** tends to be attached to the seed companies' selections.

Freshly picked Cape gooseberries displaying the protective calyx

A sturdy cane can be a useful support

MELONS

❝I can only feel sorry for melons. They are one of the plants to which no one seems willing to give a home. Vegetable growers think they are fruit because they taste sweet, while fruit growers and seed companies think they are vegetables because they are closely related to cucumbers and marrows. I simply think they are delicious and, as I tend to eat them either before or after a main course but seldom during it, as far as I am concerned they are annual soft fruit. ❞

HISTORY AND TYPES OF MELON

I don't think anyone is quite sure where the melon originated as it's now so commonly grown in all the warm areas of the world, but Africa seems the most likely place. Although they were cultivated in ancient times, it has really only been during the past 500 years or so that melons have been of any significance as food plants, probably as better, sweeter forms became available. Although all melons are of the same botanical sub-species, *Cucumis melo* ssp. *melo*, there are now three main and distinct groups:

Canteloupes Spherical or oval fruit with pronounced ridges and greenish, pink or orange flesh; includes the popular 'Ogen' melon.

Netted or musk melons Spherical fruit with net-like markings and greenish, pink or orange flesh.

Winter and honeydew melons Oval fruit with a hard, smooth rind either yellow or green in colour and

with white or pale greenish flesh.

Only canteloupes and netted melons can be grown satisfactorily in cool climates, so these are the types I have discussed here. (Water melons are botanically quite distinct but in my experience are also difficult to grow in cooler climates.)

WAYS TO GROW MELONS

Melons need around 100 days free from frost (slightly more with some varieties, slightly less with others) to grow and ripen but there must also be adequate warmth, both during the daytime and at night. In Europe, therefore, it can be difficult to grow melons reliably outdoors with no protection anywhere north of central France or, of course, at high altitudes. This leaves three options: a greenhouse, a cold frame or a cloche.

With a heated greenhouse and the facility to maintain a minimum tem-

perature of about 18°C (65°F), there is no difficulty and almost all varieties can be grown. But providing this amount of heat throughout the spring and autumn can make melon growing a very costly pastime and my advice is to select only the hardier varieties and grow them in a greenhouse maintained at a minimum of about 7°C (45°F). It's very important to keep the greenhouse well ventilated, however, and melons must have dry conditions (much drier than cucumbers need) if they are not to develop diseases.

The cold frame provides the next best option but you must have somewhere warmer to raise the plants and then somewhere to harden them off before planting; and even cold frames will only be really successful in warmer areas.

Cloches are the least satisfactory, partly because of size limitations and also because they provide less enhanced warmth. In practice, cloches will be successful only with the hardiest varieties in warmer areas; and even then, may not be effective in cool summers. Any form of cloche may be used but the best results will come from the glass high-barn pattern which retains heat well and provides good head space.

SEED SOWING AND PLANT RAISING

Melons for growing with protection should be raised in individual pots and then transplanted with minimum root disturbance. Sow the seeds on edge, about 1cm (½in) deep, two to a 9cm (3½in) pot of soil-based sowing compost. They should germinate within about five days at 21°C (70°F).

Pull out the weaker of each pair of seedlings and grow on the remainder until they have four true leaves. If they are to be planted in a cold frame or cloches, they will then require approximately 10-14 days of hardening off.

SOIL/COMPOST

Greenhouse The soil of a greenhouse border can be used for growing melons provided it is enriched with well rotted manure or compost, but if the plants show signs of wilt or root-rotting diseases, you will need to switch to some form of container growing, either 20cm (8in) diameter pots of a soil-based compost such as John Innes No. 2, or a soilless compost in growing bags.

Cold frame Dig in well rotted manure to the central part of the cold frame, or, if the frame is large enough, at positions 1m (3ft) apart. (This is where the root system will develop, so it is absolutely pointless to enrich the soil in the entire frame.) Then raise a mound or ridge of soil at each planting position about 15cm (6in) high.

Cloche Prepare the soil as for the cold frame, again preparing the planting positions 1m (3ft) apart.

PLANTING

Take care when planting not to disturb the roots in the pot ball and ensure that the compost ball is slightly proud of the surrounding soil. If stem base rotting proves to be a problem, it is worth slipping a 'collar' of plastic pipe about 3-4cm (1-1½in) diameter over the young stem. This will ensure that the stem stays dry during watering, but must be done carefully to avoid damaging the young leaves.

FEEDING AND WATERING

The soil in which you grow your melons should not be allowed to dry out, but take care not to allow pools of water to lie around the plants during cool periods as this will encourage rotting. A proprietary liquid fertilizer with a high potash content should be applied once a week after the small fruit have begun to swell.

POLLINATION, TRAINING AND SUPPORTING

Greenhouses Melons should be trained vertically. Attach a system of horizontal wires – about 2.5mm (⅒in) diameter.plastic-coated garden wire is necessary as it must later support the weight of the fruit – about 30cm (1ft) apart to the sides and roof of the greenhouse structure. Fix a vertical cane or similar support behind each plant and attach this securely to the wires.

Tie the vertical shoot to the cane and pinch out the tip once the greenhouse roof has been reached. Tie-in side-shoots along the horizontal wires and pinch out their tips once they have produced six leaves. Flowers will then form; male flowers first with no swelling and subsequently female flowers with a small swelling behind the petals. Once six or seven female flowers are fully open, they should be pollinated. Pull off a few male flowers on a warm, sunny day, and press one into each of the female flowers – don't pollinate more than three female flowers with each male.

Pinch out any further flowers that form, as the plant will be unable to ripen them all and, from now on, pay special attention to ventilation. The swelling fruits will need supporting with nets tied to the horizontal wires. Special melon nets may be bought or you can improvise with pieces of plastic fruit cage netting.

The ideal soil for growing melons is rich and well manured

MELONS

In a greenhouse set up a system of horizontal wires. Attach the plant to a secure vertical cane. Pinch out the tip once it has reached the top.

Tie in side-shoots and pinch out tips after they've produced six leaves

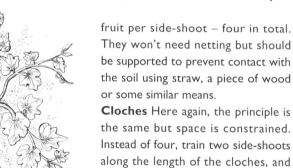

In a cold frame, pinch out tips once they have five leaves. Train the four strongest side-shoots

Cold frames The principles are the same as for greenhouse plants but instead of training one main shoot vertically, pinch out its tip when it has produced five leaves. It will then form side-shoots. You should train the four strongest along the soil towards each corner of the frame and remove the remainder. Pinch out the tips when the side-shoots reach the corners, and as the flowers develop, pollinate as before but retain only one fruit per side-shoot – four in total. They won't need netting but should be supported to prevent contact with the soil using straw, a piece of wood or some similar means.

Cloches Here again, the principle is the same but space is constrained. Instead of four, train two side-shoots along the length of the cloches, and allow each to produce a single fruit.

HARVESTING AND STORING

Melons don't ripen very satisfactorily after picking, so they should be left on the plant until mature. The end away from the stem should be slightly soft and the fruit part fairly easily from the stem when lifted. Unfortunately, they can be kept only for a few days in a fridge.

PROBLEMS

The principle problems on melons are rotting of fruit or stem, encouraged by too moist an atmosphere, soil or compost; mildew, which is

Damage to the stalk is a common way for decay fungi to enter the fruit

Canteloupe varieties

'EARLY SWEET' F₁ hybrid, early, pale orange rind, orange flesh, sweet.

*'OGEN' Early, green-yellow rind, pale green flesh, sweet and juicy but not as hardy as 'Sweetheart'.

*'SWEETHEART' F₁ hybrid, early, green-grey rind, pink-orange flesh, sweet, overall the best melon for cool greenhouse or frame and the only really reliable one for cloche growing.

'CHARANTAIS' Mid-season, small, greyish green rind, red-orange flesh, sweet in good summers, juicy.

Netted Melon varieties

'EMERALD GEM' Early to mid-season, green-orange rind, green flesh, sweet.

'GALIA' F₁ Early to mid-season, pale orange rind, green-yellow flesh, sweet.

'MINNESOTA MIDGET' Early, very compact, orange rind, orange flesh, sweet, juicy.

'AMBER NECTAR' Mid-season, yellow-orange rind with green stripes, orange flesh, sweet, said to have good disease resistance and to have been bred for cooler climates.

'ROMEO' F₁ Mid-season, pale green-grey with green stripes, orange flesh, sweet.

*'BLENHEIM ORANGE' Late, yellowish rind, red-orange flesh, sweet but really requires a warm greenhouse.

'HERO OF LOCKINGE' Late, orange rind, very pale green flesh, sweet, a good warm or cool greenhouse variety.

* my top three garden melons

fairly readily controlled by sulphur or proprietary systemic fungicide spray and virus, carried by aphids which should be controlled by contact insecticide spray as soon as they are seen. Wilt, which results in the collapse and death of the entire plant is only likely to occur when plants have been repeatedly cropped from the same greenhouse soil bed.

'Ogen'

'Sweetheart'

'Blenheim Orange'

GRAPES

66I once upset the home wine-making fraternity by saying that, as far I was concerned, wine comes from Vitis vinifera *and nothing else. Perhaps I was stretching a point to make another, but the grapevine has undeniably provided mankind with more pleasurable drinking for more years than any other plant on the planet. It is easy to grow grapevines outdoors anywhere that experiences reasonably mild winters. But to grow them well enough to produce a dessert crop needs rather more care, and while you certainly can make wine from garden-grown grapes, your main problem will be one of having room to grow enough vines to make the exercise worthwhile. I shall concentrate, therefore, on growing outdoor and greenhouse vines for modest dessert fruit production. 99*

HISTORY AND TYPES OF GRAPE

Grape growing for wine production was familiar to all of the ancient civilisations and, although the origin of the wild plant is unknown, it probably first grew in south-east Europe or south-west Asia. Grape growing spread northwards and westwards, reaching Britain and other more northerly parts of western Europe with the Romans. Since then, there have almost always been some vineyards in Britain although they have been restricted to the extreme south during periods of climatic cold. The Spaniards took vines to North America although there are native American species, most notably *Vitis labrusco*, *Vitis rotundifolia* and *Vitis aestivalis*, that have contributed particular characteristics to some modern varieties. Others have been used to develop rootstock varieties, especially those that display resistance to the root aphid-like pest *Phylloxera*. This creature virtually obliterated European vineyards in the late-nineteenth century and was overcome only by using resistant American rootstocks onto which the best and most carefully selected European varieties were grafted. Although a tragedy at the time, it forced a rigorous weeding out of old and relatively useless varieties.

SOIL

Soil for grapes must be fertile, moist and well drained. They will not thrive in very thin, impoverished soils nor in waterlogged conditions, but vines tolerate fairly high alkalinity and some of the very best grapes come from limestone sites. Paradoxically, on chalky soils, more acidic grape juice is produced. Although it is possible to grow grapevines in containers, this is is really only satisfactory when they are trained specially as standards (see p.112); full-sized vines, even those grown in greenhouses, are much better planted in the ground, preferably just outside the house with the main stem trained in through a small hole.

SITE

Grapes must have warmth. Almost all the major wine growing regions of the world lie between latitudes 30° and 50°. Whilst this embraces most of the United States, it excludes Canada, Britain and northern Europe which are too cold, and most of Africa and Australia which are too hot. Successful grape growing outdoors north of 50°N requires a locally warm, sheltered site and a south or south-west aspect, preferably fairly free from strong winds. The average summer temperature should be not less than about 19°C (66°F) and the average winter temperature not less than about -1°C (30°F). In gardens, grapevines will almost always be planted against a warm wall rather than free-standing and this is the method that I describe in the following text.

GREENHOUSES

The main requirements for grape houses are that they should face south or south-west and have sufficient head room to enable the plants to be trained properly. Both free-standing and lean-to structures are suitable, although the lean-to has the added advantage of taking warmth from the adjoining building. While a

The best soil for growing grapes is fertile, moist and well drained

heated greenhouse would enable you to grow some of the finest-flavoured dessert grapes (among the so-called Muscat and Vinous groups of varieties), I don't recommend this. They can be tricky to grow and, of course, the cost of heat towards the end of the season can be considerable. I advise choosing the more hardy varieties (p.116) for which significant heating is neither necessary nor desirable, and for which the greenhouse should ideally be maintained at a minimum temperature slightly above freezing. Good ventilation is very important to minimize mildew and fruit-rotting moulds.

PLANTING AND SPACING

Grapevines are best planted in early winter when they are fully dormant. Prepare the planting position with well rotted manure or compost and a light dressing of bone meal, and plant to the depth indicated by the soil mark on the stem. Slope the soil away from the base of the stem after planting and top up with a mulch of compost, leaf mould or manure. The planting position should be 20-25cm (8-10in) away from the wall. Greenhouse vines are best planted in exactly the same way but just outside one end of the house then trained in through a hole in the wall. In most gardens and certainly in most greenhouses, there will be space for only one plant; grapevines are self-fertile so fruit production won't be affected. Against a long wall outdoors however, where two or more plants could be grown, they should be spaced 2m (6ft) apart.

GRAPES

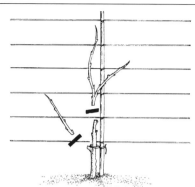

After planting, cut the main stem to 60-75cm (24-30in) and the laterals to two buds from the base

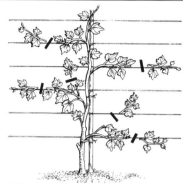

Tie strongest side-shoots to the horizontal wires, pinch out beyond five leaves. Pinch out other shoots

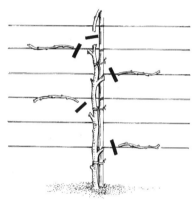

In the following winter, cut back main shoot by half, cut back laterals to two buds from base

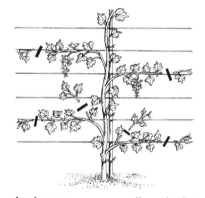

In the next summer, allow the laterals to bear fruit and pinch out at two leaves beyond the fruit bunch

A strong system of wires supports this fruit-laden vine very well

SUPPORTS, TRAINING AND PRUNING

The support for vines must be robust, as a plant in full leaf and fruit is both heavy and bulky. Against a vertical wall, horizontal wires should be used, spaced 30cm (12in) apart up to the top of the wall and anchored with vine eyes screwed in to wall plugs. Use 10 gauge – 3.15mm (⅛in) diameter – plastic-coated training wire. In a greenhouse, the wires will need to be stretched along the length of the side walls of the house and also continued up the roof slope, secured to the glazing bars.

There are numerous systems for training grapevines, some developed for particular varieties, but I have found much the simplest, both in greenhouses and outdoors to be a basic cordon or simple espalier method. This is the system I have explained here. It is easy to understand (which is more than can be said for some of the commercial techniques), easily done and gives good, heavy crops.

OUTDOORS AGAINST A WALL

Immediately after planting, cut the main stem down to about 60-75cm (24-30in) above soil level, cutting to just above a bud. Insert a stout bamboo cane close to the plant, secure the cane to the wires and tie the vine stem to the cane. In the first season, tie the main stem vertically to the cane and pinch out its top when it reaches the topmost wire. Side-shoots will develop and the strongest of these should be tied to the horizontal wires to the right and left of the main stem (or rod as we should

Ideally, grapevines grown outdoors should be sited against a wall to receive maximum sun and warmth

GRAPES

When growing a grapevine in a container you are unlikely to obtain a very large crop, and it should be viewed more as an ornamental plant

GROWING STANDARD GRAPEVINES IN CONTAINERS

This is an attractive, if not very productive way of growing grapes but is both useful and interesting for conservatories, although careful attention must be paid to pest and disease control. It was a very popular method in Victorian times when entire potted plants were brought into dining rooms for guests to pick their own fresh fruit.

Use a terracotta pot of about 40cm (16in) diameter with a soil-based compost such as John Innes No. 3. A single stem is trained vertically, supported by a stout cane, to a height of about 1.2m (4ft). Six lateral shoots are allowed to develop from the apex (all others are rubbed out) and pinched out beyond the flower cluster, just as with normal vine pruning (p.110). The lateral shoots are allowed to droop downwards and are supported by soft string tied to the top of the support cane. Each winter, the lateral shoots are pruned back to two buds from their bases. As with any container-grown plant, careful attention must be given to ensure that the compost doesn't dry out and a high potash liquid feed should be given every two weeks during the growing season.

now call it). These side-shoots should be pinched out at a point just beyond five leaves from their base. All the other side-shoots should be pinched out.

In the following winter, cut back the main shoot by approximately half and cut back the lateral shoots to about 2-5cm (1-2in) from their bases.

The next season, the process is more or less repeated and you should, once more, only allow a single lateral shoot to develop from each of the stubs; carefully pinch out the weaker ones. In the second winter, cut back the lateral shoots again, and again shorten the main shoot – it will, of course, gradually be getting

closer to the top of the cane.

In subsequent years, flowers and fruit can be expected but it's important not to be too greedy and allow too many to develop, as the individual bunches and fruit will be small. One per lateral shoot is ideal in the first year, two in the second and three in subsequent years. The shoot

A healthy greenhouse vine with the laterals spreading out along the structure

GRAPES

should, therefore, be pinched back to a point just above three leaves beyond the first, second or third flower cluster as appropriate. Side-shoots will then form from the laterals and these should be pinched out at just beyond one leaf.

In the winter, the laterals should be cut back regularly to leave short stubs and, when the main rod has reached the end of its allotted space, it too should be treated just like a lateral and cut back to the same point each winter.

GREENHOUSES

With a vine planted just outside a greenhouse, the main shoot should first be passed into the house through a hole cut into the end wall close to soil level. Thereafter, the basic training and pruning is similar to that employed on outdoor vines, but the main rod must be directed along the greenhouse structure as explained below.

In a lean-to greenhouse, direct the rod up the side wall and then along the angle formed where the bottom edge of the roof meets the wall. The laterals are, in turn, directed up the slope of the roof. In a free-standing span house, the same system may be adopted, or else the rod may be pinched out when it reaches the top of the wall and so encouraged to branch. In this case, one branch is trained as before while the other is taken across the end wall and trained along the opposite side, effectively producing a two-armed cordon with the two sets of laterals tied up the two roof slopes and meeting at the ridge. Thereafter, the pruning is exactly as I've described for outdoor vines.

If you are growing grapes for dessert use, rather than for wine making, it's important to thin out the fruit within the bunches so that the individual grapes will be large and plump. Use blunt-ended scissors and work upwards from the bottom of each bunch, snipping out about half of the grapes when they are around 5mm (¼in) in diameter.

FEEDING AND WATERING

The soil in which you grow your vines shouldn't be allowed to dry out while the fruit are swelling, and so the plants should be mulched in autumn and spring and then watered copiously in the summer. Give about 34g per square metre (1oz per square yard) of a balanced general fertilizer such as Growmore or fish, blood and bone in spring and a proprietary liquid feed with high potash content every two weeks during the summer.

YIELDS

Yields and fruit quality will vary enormously with the warmth of the climate, care given to pruning, feeding and watering, the choice of variety and, of course, the space available. From a mature vine, well

A fine powder covers the leaves and fruit when beset with powdery mildew

cared for and trained as a double cordon in a standard-sized 3 x 2.5m (10 x 8ft) greenhouse, it should be possible to obtain at least 50-60 bunches.

HARVESTING AND STORING

It's almost impossible to tell by appearance whether grapes are ripe or not and much the best way is to test a single fruit to see if it tastes agreeably sweet. They should then be cut in bunches, not individually, with either scissors or snips. Cut out a short length of the shoot on which the bunch is borne to give a T-shaped 'handle' at the end of the bunch stalk. The grapes will keep fresh for about a week at room temperature or for about two weeks in a refrigerator.

A popular old method of storing involved special horizontal grape bottles, filled with water. The bunches were cut with much longer sections of branch attached, the branch was placed through the narrow neck of the bottle into the water and the grapes allowed to lie adjacent. In this way, and in the dark, the bunches kept fresh for several weeks and a similar system could be improvized today. Grapes can be frozen fairly satisfactorily but it is an extremely fiddly process, for each fruit must be sliced and the pips removed.

PROBLEMS

By far the biggest problems on grapevines are mildew and botrytis grey mould. Both are especially troublesome in greenhouses, and both are best combated by ensuring that, through adequate ventilation and pruning, the plants have a decent free flow of air around them. The following notes should be read in conjunction with my general remarks on pp.30-31.

MAIN SYMPTOMS	CAUSE	TREATMENT
Fruit		
Partially eaten, contents may be removed	Wasps	Difficult; fine netting over greenhouse windows and door may help to exclude insects but little can be done outdoors
Rotted, fluffy grey mould present	Botrytis grey mould	Improve greenhouse ventilation, spray with sulphur or systemic fungicide
Leaves		
Powdery white coating	Powdery mildew	Spray with sulphur or systemic fungicide
Pale yellow spots with whitish mould beneath	Downy mildew	Spray with copper-containing fungicide immediately before and after flowering; repeat 10 and 20 days later
Sticky black coating aphids	Sooty mould	Use contact insecticide to control which produce honeydew on which the mould grows (see also scale insects)
Mottled or distorted	Virus	No treatment feasible
Bronzed or yellow, often drop prematurely	Red spider mites	No chemical control possible, maintain good ventilation and a moist atmosphere in greenhouses
Yellow or brown waxy scales, often on stems too and with black, sticky mould	Scale insects	Use a stiff brush on stems to remove loose bark in winter and apply a tar oil spray when plants are fully dormant
Stems		
Tiny patches of waxy 'wool' with woodlouse-like insects beneath (on greenhouse plants)	Mealybugs	Spray with contact insecticide and apply tar oil spray in winter

GRAPES Varieties

The number of grape varieties in the world is legion. Most have been raised for wine production, and as any wine connoisseur will know, the juice from different varieties will result in wines of greatly differing character. There are many fewer varieties grown for dessert fruit production and fewer still that are suitable for greenhouse or outdoor cultivation in climatically marginal growing areas. It is the hardier dessert types that I list here. There are both black and white varieties, but while some types are suitable only for outdoor cultivation, others can be grown both outdoors and in greenhouses, while there are some that can only be grown indoors. Among the latter, the Sweetwater grapes are the easiest and most reliable, managing to ripen early before the temperature begins to drop in autumn. All other types of greenhouse grape really need some heat in the latter part of the season if they are to ripen successfully and for that reason, I don't recommend them.

'Pirovano 14'

'Buckland Sweetwater'

*'**BLACK HAMBURGH**' (also called 'Schiava Grossa') Black, greenhouse, early to mid-season, heavy cropping, good flavour.

'**BUCKLAND SWEETWATER**' White, greenhouse, early, moderate cropping, moderate flavour.

'**CHASSELAS**' Black (but pale pinkish fruit), greenhouse, early, moderate cropping, moderate flavour.

*'**FOSTER'S SEEDLING**' White, greenhouse, early, heavy cropping, good flavour.

'**LEON MILLOT**' Black, outdoor, mid-season, fairly heavy cropping but small bunches, fairly good disease resistance, good flavour.

'**MADELEINE ANGEVINE**' White, outdoor, early, heavy cropping, moderate flavour.

'**MADELEINE SYLVANER**' White, outdoor, early, moderate cropping, moderate flavour.

'**MULLER-THURGAU**' White, outdoor, mid-season, moderate cropping (good in warm years), moderate flavour and best as a wine grape.

'**PIROVANO 14**' Black, outdoor, early, heavy cropping, good flavour.

*'**SIEGERREBE**' White, outdoor, early, heavy cropping, good flavour.

* my top three garden or cool greenhouse grapes

'Foster's Seedling'

'Chasselas'

'Madeleine Angevine'

'Muller-Thurgau'

'Siegerrebe'

'Black Hamburgh'

KIWI FRUIT

❝ They're clever folk, the New Zealanders. They took a plant that we'd always known as the Chinese gooseberry, Actinidia deliciosa *and discovered that its fruit have just the qualities needed for a commercial crop: they can be eaten in any number of ways, with sweets or savouries, the plants are easy to grow, very hardy, crop abundantly and, most importantly for a faraway country, they store and travel very well. The final touch was to do away with the old name, rechristen them Kiwi fruit and you had the best thing to hit New Zealand since sheep. They caught on in European supermarkets and, of course, gardeners then wanted to grow them at home. And there's no real reason why they shouldn't. They are about as hardy as grapevines and are pruned rather similarly too. ❞*

HISTORY AND TYPES OF KIWI FRUIT

As its old common name suggests, *Actinidia deliciosa* (which you will still sometimes see listed as *Actinidia chinensis*) is a Chinese plant, originally seen in the wild by the great plant collector, Robert Fortune, in 1847 although it wasn't cultivated in the West until the early part of the twentieth century. It was introduced to New Zealand at about the same time but for many years, no one took much interest in it. And although it first began to be grown commercially in New Zealand in the 1930s, its success as a major crop dates from the 1960s. In recent

Ripe, succulent and ready-to-eat

years, a great deal of selection and breeding and also studies of the best cultivation methods have been carried out, but New Zealand no longer has it all its own way and several other countries are now growing Kiwi fruit commercially.

SOIL

The soil must be moist but with no tendency to waterlogging, ideally rich in humus and very slightly acid, although Kiwi fruit will tolerate moderate alkalinity if this is countered with applications of sequestered iron fertilizer. Very heavy or very light soils must be improved with organic matter and as Kiwi fruit are commonly planted against walls, it must be borne in mind that the soil in such positions will normally be quite dry and impoverished.

SITE

Kiwi fruit will tolerate about -15°C (5°F) in winter but the young shoots and flowers are likely to be damaged by even fairly light spring frosts, so a sheltered position is essential in all except the very mildest areas. The branches are also rather brittle, an additional reason for providing shelter from winds. A position against a south or south-west facing wall is ideal and, although Kiwi fruit can be grown in the open against wires, this method can only be relied on in warm and sunny climates.

Kiwi fruit can, of course, be grown in greenhouses but they are so vigorous that you really do need a large greenhouse to do this successfully, and you would have to accept that there would be very little room for anything else. My view is that, if your climate isn't mild enough to grow them outdoors, they can be more trouble than they are worth.

PLANTING

I prefer to plant in the early autumn, when the plants should have a chance to establish properly before the winter, or, better still, in mid-spring, when the worst of the cold weather has passed. *Actinidia* are almost always sold in containers, not bare-rooted and should be planted up to the soil mark on the stem, in a planting position prepared with organic matter and a dressing of bone meal. Firm them in well and slope the soil away from the plant, finally topping up with a mulch of compost.

SPACING

Kiwi fruits are very vigorous plants. Almost all the varieties are also unisexual and so must have a partner

The fruit will only set if the flowers escape frost damage, so care must be taken when siting the plant

for pollination. Even in a limited space, therefore, you will generally need two plants and they are sometimes sold with a male and female in the same pot. They should then be planted as one, in the same planting hole, the shoots subsequently being trained in opposite directions. Sometimes, it may be possible to buy female plants on to which a male branch has been grafted. Where space allows you to grow more plants, allow one male for every five females and space them about 6m (20ft) apart. Where plants are grown against a wall, plant them about 20-25cm (8-10in) away from the wall itself. Where they are grown with free-standing wires (see below), plant them in line with the support posts.

SUPPORTS AND TRAINING

Against a wall, use a system of horizontal wires, attached to vine eyes, screwed to wall plugs. You will need 10 gauge – 3.15mm (⅛in) diameter – plastic-coated wire, and spaced 45cm (18in) apart to a height of 2m (6ft). In mild areas and given the room, a free-standing system of wires may be used. Erect supports similar to those used for the Worcester system of growing raspberries (p.40) with two vertical, braced posts about 6m (20ft) apart and with top cross pieces 1m (3ft) across. Fix three, not two wires, one in the centre, in line with the centre posts and one, as with raspberries, at the end of each cross-piece.

PRUNING

Against a wall After planting, cut back the main stem to just above the lowest wire and tie it to the wire. As new shoots arise, tie one vertically and two laterally along the wires, and cut out any others. As the main centre shoot grows upwards, tie it to the next wire and repeat the lateral training with two more shoots. Repeat the process until the top wire is reached. When the lateral shoots are about 1m (3ft) long, pinch out their tips. This will encourage side-shoots to form and these in turn should be pinched out just above five leaves from the base. By the third year, some of these side-shoots will bear fruit and so become fruiting spurs. These should be pinched out at five leaves beyond the fruit cluster. Those that don't should be pinched out five leaves above the base. In the winter, all of the side shoots should be cut back; either to two buds from the base, if they didn't fruit, or to two buds beyond where the fruit developed, if they did. The process is then repeated in subsequent years.

KIWI FRUIT

It is important not to allow the plants to dry out once the fruit begins to swell, so water freely during this period

should be tied laterally across the wires in pairs at intervals of about 45cm (18in), any others being cut out. Pinch out the tips of the side-shoots. Continue with this process until the wire framework is covered. Fruiting spurs will develop and hang downwards from the side-shoots and these should be treated in the same way as on wall-trained plants. In both pruning systems, wayward shoots that arise elsewhere on the plants should be cut out promptly.

FEEDING AND WATERING

In early spring, give the plants 34g per square metre (1oz per square yard) of Growmore or fish, blood and bone; follow this with a mulch of well rotted compost. Ensure that the soil does not dry out in the spring and early summer but be careful not to overwater in the final stages of fruit swelling. This is different from the watering of most other fruits but it is important to ensure that the ripening process takes place slowly.

Fruit set will be improved if you assist with pollination by using a very soft brush to remove the pollen from the male flowers and dust it

On free-standing wires After planting, cut back the main stem to a height of about 60cm (24in) and insert a firm cane or stake next to each plant. Tie the stem to the support and, as new shoots develop, select the strongest and train it up the cane, cutting out all others. When the main stem reaches the wire, pinch it out. Again more shoots will arise; select the two strongest and train them along the centre wire. Pinch out all other shoots. Side-shoots will arise from the two and

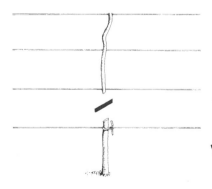

After planting, cut back the main stem to about 60cm (24in)

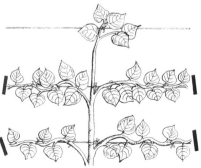

Select the strongest shoots and tie one vertically and two laterally along the wires

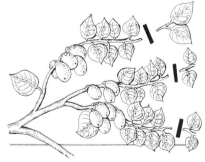

When lateral shoots are 1m (3ft) long pinch out their tips

Female (fruiting) varieties

'ABBOTT' Early flowering so rather prone to frost damage, heavy cropping, medium sized fruit.

'BRUNO' Early flowering so rather prone to frost damage, heavy cropping, large, dark brown fruit.

*'HAYWARD' Late flowering, misses much frost damage, heavy cropping, large pale brown fruit.

Male (pollinating) varieties

Any variety will suffice but the ones seen most commonly are **'MATUA'**, **'TOMURI'**, **'ATLAS'** (which clearly has ideas beyond its station) and the soberly named **'ALL PURPOSE'**.

Self-fertile variety

'BLAKE' Early flowering, moderate cropping, small to medium sized fruit.

* my top fruiting Kiwi fruit

n.b. You may occasionally see seed or seedling plants for sale. Don't waste time and money with them; they will not come true to type, you will need to wait until they flower to discover their sex and they will be most unlikely to produce any worthwhile fruit.

'Abbott'

'Bruno'

'Hayward'

into the females. One male flower should produce sufficient pollen for about five females.

WEEDING

The mulch around the plants should control most annual weeds but perennial weeds can be hoed. The root system is not very shallow and hoeing is unlikely to damage it.

YIELDS AND NUMBERS OF PLANTS NEEDED

The number of plants is likely to be dictated by space but an established wall-trained plant on a wall about 2m (6ft) high and about 3m (10ft) wide should produce about 50-100 fruits.

HARVESTING AND STORING

It's easy to tell when the fruits are ripe because they are slightly soft when pressed and snap very easily from the stalk. As I've already mentioned, they store well, keeping for about two weeks at room temperature and for about three months in a refrigerator. Harvest all fruit, ripe and unripe, before the first frosts and then ripen them gradually in warmth indoors.

PROBLEMS

The only problems likely to arise are red spider mites, aphids or caterpillars and these are seldom serious.

GLOSSARY OF TERMS

A

ACID describes soils with pH of less than 7.0

ACID-SOIL FRUIT fruit that will only grow on acid soils

ALKALINE describes soils with pH of more than 7.0

ANNUAL plant completing its life-cycle from seed to seed in one season

APEX tip of a root or shoot

B

BARE-ROOTED describes plants lifted from nursery beds with little or no soil on the roots. Most bush and cane fruit is supplied in this form

BONE MEAL source of fairly slow-release phosphorus

BORDEAUX MIXTURE fungicide mixture of copper sulphate and lime

C

CALYX outer protective parts of flower or fruit

CANE slender, woody stem. Applied to raspberries, blackberries and hybrid berries

CHLOROPHYLL green pigment in plants responsible for photosynthesis

CHLOROSIS loss of chlorophyll, resulting in yellowing leaves

COMPOST potting medium, or material made of decomposed plant remains

CONTAINER-GROWN describes plant raised and sold in a pot, as opposed to bare-rooted

CORDON plant restricted to a single stem by pruning. Double and triple cordons have two and three stems respectively

CROSS-POLLINATION transfer of pollen from one flower to the stigma of another flower of the same type

CROWN a compressed stem base from which roots and shoots grow

CUTTINGS parts of a plant cut off to be used for propagating other plants with identical characteristics

D

DAY-NEUTRAL describes a plant, the flowering of which is not dictated by day length

DIEBACK death of shoot tips caused by damage or disease

DORMANT describes the resting period, usually winter, when plants make little or no growth

DRIED BLOOD fast-acting organic source of nitrogen

E

ERICACEOUS when applied to compost, suitable for lime-hating plants

ESPALIER form of training in which a vertical trunk has one or more pairs of branches emerging from it on opposite sides

F

FAMILY category of botanical classification grouping together plants of different but related genera

FAN form of training in which several shoots are encouraged to radiate out from a central leg in a fan shape

FILLIS soft string for tying plants to supports

FISH, BLOOD AND BONE balanced fertilizer, containing nitrogen, phosphorus and potash

FRAMEWORK permanent, trained structure of shoots or branches

FREE-STANDING growing without support

FRUITED having produced fruit

G

GENUS (pl. genera) category in botanical classification that groups together a number of allied species

GRAFT a union created from the stem of one plant and the root of another

GROWMORE established formula of balanced artificial fertilizer containing nitrogen, phosphorus and potassium in the approximate ratio 7:7:7

H

HARDEN-OFF to acclimatize indoor-raised plants to outdoor conditions

HEELED-IN temporarily planted

HYBRID plant derived by crossing two distinct species or varieties

J

JOHN INNES No2, No3 composts soil-based composts with established formulae for medium to long-term raising of plants in containers

L

LATERAL shoot arising from a main branch or stem

LEADER growing tip of a main branch

LEAF MOULD decomposed leaves

LEG main stem of a fruit bush

LOAM type of soil, usually quite fertile, containing clay, silt, sand and humus

M

MICRO-PROPAGATION propagation using tissue culture

MULCH material spread over soil

N

NUTRIENTS minerals taken up by roots, and used in plant growth

O

ORGANIC MATTER composts or manures, based on decomposed plant matter

P

pH measurement of soil acidity. pH7 is said to be neutral, above is alkaline, below is acid

PINCHING OUT removal of growing tip, intended to encourage production of side-shoots

PLUG hard centre of a raspberry

POLLINATION transfer of pollen from anther to stigma, essential for fruit development

PREDATOR INSECTS beneficial insects, such as ladybirds, hoverflies and lacewings, that eat pests

PROPAGATION increase of plants

PROPAGATOR structure providing warm and humid atmosphere intended to favour seedlings and cuttings

PRUNING systematic removal of dead, diseased or otherwise unwanted woody stems

R

REMONTANT flowering and, therefore, fruiting at intervals throughout the growing season

REVERSION return to original (usually undesirable) state

ROD main stem of a grape vine

ROOT-BALL roots and soil seen when plant is removed from container

ROOTSTOCK plant providing roots for another plant of the same variety, which is grafted on to it

ROTATION systematic change of location for a crop, intended to prevent build up of soil pests and diseases

RUNNERS small plantlets arising from a strawberry plant

S

SELF-FERTILE describes a plant that can be successfully fertilized with its own pollen

SET fertilization leading to production of fruit

SIDE-SHOOTS shoots or branches arising from a main stem

SOIL-BASED describes a compost based on loam

SOILLESS describes a compost based on peat or other organic material

SPECIES category in botanical classification, directly below genus, containing closely related, similar plants

SPUR short lateral branch with a number of buds

STANDARD plant with at least 2m (6ft) of bare stem below first branches; half-standard must have clear stem of 1-1.2m (3-4ft)

STOLON prostrate, creeping stem giving rise to plantlets

STOOL clump of shoots

STRAINING WIRE strong garden wire, usually 10 gauge

STRAWBERRY MATS squares of plastic sheeting placed beneath strawberry plants as fruits ripen to prevent contact with soil and protect against slugs

STRIG stem bearing currant berries

SULPHATE OF AMMONIA (ammonium sulphate) source of nitrogen

SULPHATE OF POTASH (potassium sulphate) source of potassium

SYSTEMIC describes a chemical (usually pesticide or herbicide) that is carried through the plant after application

T

TAR OIL (winter wash) spray used only on dormant, deciduous woody plants to destroy overwintering insect pests

THINNING-OUT systematic removal of fruits to improve size and quality of those remaining

TIP-LAYERING form of propagation in which new plants are formed at the tip of a flexible stem when it comes in contact with soil

TRANSLOCATED see systemic

V

VARIETIES naturally occurring variants of a species

W

WILT collapse of plant due to disease

INDEX

PHOTOGRAPHIC ACKNOWLEDGEMENTS

Front cover: Boys Syndication **Back cover**: Dr S T Buczacki

Inside photographs

Amateur Gardening 21 right, 60 top, 83 bottom right, 85 left, 94 top, 96 top left, 96 bottom left, 117 centre left
Sue Atkinson 22 right, 27, 34, 43, 51, 53, 55, 64, 81, 92, 103 left, 118; A-Z Botanical Collection 59 top left,
71 centre left; Harry Baker 109, 117 top left; Boys Syndication 6 top, 84 top, 87, 91 right; Pat Brindley 38 bottom, 67,
80, 107 bottom; Brogdale Horticultural Trust 46 bottom, 47 centre right, 48 top left, 48 centre left, 48 bottom left,
48 top right, 48 bottom right, 49 left, 59 bottom centre, 59 bottom right, 70 bottom, 71 top left, 71 bottom left,
72 bottom, 73 top left, 73 bottom centre, 82 top, 83 bottom centre, 83 top right, 85 top right, 94 centre, 94 bottom,
95 top left, 95 top centre, 95 top right, 95 centre right, 95 bottom left, 95 bottom right, 96 centre left,
96 bottom centre, 96 bottom right; Dr S T Buczacki 84 bottom, 93; Collections/Patrick Johns 61; Eric Crichton 70 top;
Fleurmerc bv 58 top, 98 top, 100 centre; Liz Gibbons/Natural Image 6 bottom; John Glover 59 top right,
100 bottom left, 100 right, 110 bottom; Jill Hedges Garden Archive 36, 50, 62, 74 top, 86, 104, 108; Holt Studios
International/John Adams 117 top centre, /Nigel Cattlin 30 top, 30 bottom, 31, 54, 56, 57 right, 63, 69 left, 90, 102, 105,
120 top, /John Henry Galindo 98 bottom, /Rosemary Mayer 19, 26, 78 top, /Primrose Peacock 41, /Duncan Smith 119;
Andrew Lawson 20 top, 21 left, 79; Oxford Scientific Films/Gordon Maclean 107 top; Photos Horticultural 3, 10, 11, 12
left, 13, 16,17 top left, 17 bottom right, 20 bottom, 22 left, 23 bottom, 24 right, 32, 33, 35, 37 bottom, 42, 44,
47 top right, 47 centre left, 49 top right, 52, 58 centre, 58 bottom, 59 bottom left, 59 top centre, 59 centre, 60 bottom,
69 right, 71 centre right, 71 bottom right, 72 top, 73 top right, 74 bottom, 75, 82 centre, 82 bottom, 83 top left,
83 top centre, 85 centre right, 85 bottom right, 91 left, 97 bottom right, 99, 107 centre, 112, 113, 114, 116 top,
116 bottom, 117 top right, 117 bottom left; Reed International Picture Library/Michael Boys 25,/Jerry Harper 29
top,/Jerry Harper and Bob Flowerdew 15, 28; Scottish Crop Research Institute 38 top, 45, 57 left; Clive Simms 7, 101
left, 101 right, 117 bottom right, 121 bottom; Harry Smith Collection 9, 12 right, 23 top, 24 left,
29 bottom, 37 top, 46 top, 47 top left, 47 bottom left, 47 bottom right, 49 centre right, 49 bottom right, 65, 68,
71 top right, 73 bottom right, 83 bottom left, 85 centre, 89, 95 centre left, 95 centre, 100 top left, 103 right, 106,
111, 117 centre right, 121 top; Suttons Seeds 97 top; Thompson & Morgan 97 bottom left; Visions 73 bottom left,
121 centre; Elizabeth Whiting Associates 8.

TEMPERATURE CHART		
BARELY HARDY	0 to -5°C	32 to 23°F
FAIRLY HARDY	-5 to -10°C	23 to 14°F
MODERATELY HARDY	-10 to -15°C	14 to 5°F
HARDY	-15 to -20°C	5 to -4°F
VERY HARDY	-20°C or below	-4°F or below

G Amateur GARDENING

OTHER TITLES AVAILABLE:

Best Climbers
Best Foliage Shrubs
Best Shade Plants

To be published Spring 1995:

Best Water Gardening
Best Herbs

Hamlyn, in association with **Amateur Gardening** also publish a handy Pocket Reference series in a wipe-clean plastic wallet. titles available:

The Hellyer Pocket Guide
by Arthur Hellyer MBE VMH
Gardener's Fact Finder
Edited by Graham Clarke

These books are available from all good bookshops or by mail order direct from the Publisher. Payment can be made by credit card or cheque/postal order in the following ways:

BY PHONE

Phone through your order on our special CREDIT CARD HOTLINE on 0933 410511, quoting reference DPN. Speak to our customer service team during office hours (9am to 5pm) or leave a message on the answer machine, quoting your full credit card number, plus expiry date, and your full name and address.

BY POST

Simply fill out the order form below and send it to:
REED BOOK SERVICES LTD, PO BOX 5, RUSHDEN, NORTHANTS, NN10 6YX

I wish to order the following titles

		Price	Quantity	Total	Postage and packing	£1.00
The Hellyer Pocket Guide ISBN 0 600 57698 1	£4.99					
Gardener's Fact Finder ISBN 0 600 57697 3	£4.99					
Best Climbers ISBN 0 600 57732 5	£4.99					
Best Foliage Shrubs ISBN 0 600 57735 X	£4.99					
Best Shade Plants ISBN 0 600 57734 1	£4.99					
Best Soft Fruit ISBN 0 600 57733 3	£4.99					

Grand total £ _____

Name _____ (block capitals)

Address _____

Postcode _____

I enclose a cheque/postal order for £ _____
made payable to **Reed Book Services Ltd**

or please debit my Access ☐ Visa ☐ AmEx ☐ Diners ☐

Number ☐☐☐☐ ☐☐☐☐ ☐☐☐☐ ☐☐☐

by £ _____ Expiry date ☐☐ ☐☐ Signature _____

Offer available to UK only   While every effort is made to keep prices low, the publisher reserves the right to increase prices at short notice. Your order will be dispatched within 28 days, subject to availability

Registered office Michelin House, 81 Fulham Road, London SW3 6RB. Registered in England No 1974080